Titles in this Series

Adventures of Richard Wagner

Edward MacDowell and His Cabin in the Pines

Frederic Chopin, Son of Poland, Early Years

Frederic Chopin, Son of Poland, Later Years

Franz Schubert and His Merry Friends

Handel at the Court of Kings

Joseph Haydn, The Merry Little Peasant

Ludwig Beethoven and the Chiming Tower Bells

Mozart, The Wonder Boy

Paganini, Master of Strings

Peter Tchaikovsky and the Nutcracker Ballet

Robert Schumann and Mascot Ziff

Sebastian Bach, The Boy from Thuringia

Stephen Foster and His Little Dog Tray

The Story of Peter Tchaikovsky

The Young Brahms

PAGANINI
Master of Strings

By

Opal Wheeler

Illustrated by Henry S. Gillette

Zeezok PUBLISHING

Paganini, Master of Strings
Written by Opal Wheeler

Originally published by E.P. Dutton & Company, New York, 1950.
Copyright © 1950, by Opal Wheeler.

ISBN 978-1-61006-013-4
Copyright © 2011 by Zeezok Publishing, LLC
Published January, 2011
Printed in the United States of America

Zeezok Publishing, LLC
PO Box 1960 • Elyria, OH 44036
info@Zeezok.com

www.Zeezok.com

PAGANINI
MASTER OF STRINGS

CHAPTER ONE

A gusty wind whirled the gray mist into a mighty curtain and chased it away, high over the blue waters of the Mediterranean Sea. And what a busy harbor of Genoa it left behind!

Fish peddlers were everywhere, hurrying to fill their baskets for the day. Deck hands, shouting and laughing noisily, loaded the boats along the waterfront with brawny arms. Over all, market bells clanged a rousing good morning.

In the bustling throng, five-year-old Nicolo darted here and there, his slender face anxious as he searched for his good friend.

"Romano! Where are you, Romano?" he called, his brown toes slipping and sliding over the wet cobbles as he ran toward the wharf.

Squirming his way through the busy group at the water's edge, his dark eyes lighted as he spied the old fisherman at the bottom of his boat, the silvery new catch heaped high at his feet.

"Beauties they are!" he was shouting to the crowd of buyers. "The best to come in for many a day!"

"Beauties!" echoed Nicolo in ringing tones. "Five for a copper!"

A shout of laughter came from the peddlers as they watched the pale-faced little visitor, trying to help with the sale.

In a few minutes the fish were gone, and Nicolo sat contentedly beside his good friend, his short legs dangling happily over the edge of the dock.

"So, little shadow!" The weathered man of the sea wrinkled his long nose in pleasure. "Early you are this morning."

Nicolo frowned, screwing his small face into a knot.

"It's the bells, Romano, waking me with their noise. If only they would sing in tune!" he sighed.

Raising his shaggy head, he listened to their rousing clatter. How harshly they clanged through the market square! Creeping closer to his friend, Nicolo buried his face in the old woolen jacket, glad of the comforting strong arm around him.

Suddenly he sat up, alert, thoughts racing through his mind.

"Romano! When I am as big as you, I will make new bells, all of shining silver!" he declared. His face was alight now as he went on with his plan, his voice lowered to a whisper. "And at night, I will climb the dark stairs and hang them in the high tower. Then in the morning, the beautiful tones will ring all over Genoa. And the people will run from their houses, and they will say, 'See what Nicolo Paganini has done!' "

Romano smiled and patted the short legs, swinging now in perfect time to the peddler's cry behind them:

"Fish ... Fresh Fish.... In the oven, in the pot, ..
Fish for Mom and Fish for Pop! ... Fresh Fish.... !"

In an instant, Nicolo was stalking behind the ragged man, piping in exact tones his catchy tune. Then, with a merry laugh, he waved back at Romano.

"Good-bye! Good-bye! I'll come again tomorrow!" he called, flying home over the damp cobbles, just two streets away.

As he rounded the corner, his sharp ears caught the sound of singing. Music! Faster sped his short little legs. Nothing in all the world did he like as much as music!

"Fu-ni-cu-li, fu-ni-cu-la!" The rollicking song danced to meet him. There in the doorway sat his father, singing at the top of his voice, accompanying himself on his old mandolin. No wonder the neighbors had gathered around, to clap and sway to the lilting music.

In the noisy, laughing throng, Nicolo spied his mother.

"Ah, my little flyaway," she welcomed him quietly, smoothing his tangled locks with work-reddened fingers. "Holiday today, and forgetting it you were!"

She looked into the delicate little face and sighed.

"He has always been pale, my Nico," she explained to a neighbor woman. "It was measles that attacked him when he was little bigger than a rabbit. And I thought it was the end,

when one morning the life seemed to have gone out. So I laid him on the bed and wept for the little one that had left us."

Nicolo never tired of hearing this story about himself, and he leaned against his mother's coarse skirt, his eyes as large as the neighbor woman's as the tale went on.

"Ah yes," Teresa's soft voice continued, "the prayers were all said for the wee mite, lying there so white and still. And then before my very eyes, there was a slight stir, and the tiny lips opened in faint crying. So we said our prayers all over again for this child that was spared to us."

"Tsch! Tsch! Tsch! A miracle!" breathed the neighbor woman.

"A miracle, indeed," agreed Teresa, patting the dark head and saying an extra little prayer of thanks.

Feeling in her apron pocket, she bent over the small boy.

"See, Nico," she whispered. "I have saved something for you. Quickly, –around the corner where you can enjoy it in peace."

A cake! In an instant, short legs had sped to a safe hiding place among the fish barrels in the musty alleyway. Never did anything taste so good, but as Nicolo munched away on the sweet morsel, his sharp ears listened hungrily to every note of the music.

The last crumb disappeared, and he bounded back to the group just as the rousing song ended. With a cry of pain, he clapped his hands over his ears.

"The music does not please you, small one?" cried his father, mopping his face with a large red handkerchief.

All eyes were on Nicolo as he answered slowly, "No, sir. It was the last note, sir."

"The last note, child?"

"Yes, Father, it was sick. Very sick."

For a moment, Antonio Paganini was speechless. Then hearty laughter chased away the frown.

"So! A young Mozart we have here!" he cried.

Mozart! Much fame and fortune the great composer had brought his family with his music, even as a small boy. A smile brightened Antonio's round face.

"Young man," he declared solemnly, "Today you begin to study music."

"Music! Music!" piped Nicolo, his feet twinkling in a merry dance. "Today is the day for music!"

That very evening, after his simple meal of bread dipped in a bit of soup, the small student moved to a place on the bench beside his father. In the light of the smoky oil lamp, his short fingers pressed down on the strings of the mandolin in simple chords, his older brother, Lucca, close at his side. At the sound of a wrong note, a sharp cry rang through the kitchen.

"No sick notes, eh boy?" laughed Antonio. In amazement, he watched the right hand busy with the pick while the tiny left finger moved swiftly up or down the string to correct the tone. How keen his ears were!

And now, every morning early, before beginning his work of cleaning the streets and loading olives on the boats, Antonio taught his son what he knew of music.

Before long, a small violin found its way into the poor home, and crying out in delight, Nicolo raised it to his shoulder. Drawing the bow over the strings, he coaxed smooth, sweet tones to flow into the room.

"Bravo!" cried Antonio. "Another Mozart is in the making!"

In a short time, Nicolo was playing simple pieces and melodies of his own composing. And so well did he work at his lessons, that on the morning when he was six, his father brought a heavy hand down on his knee.

"Wife, the boy is ready," he declared. "Put on him a red coat, and he shall play at the house doors of the town. The coins will come in handy, eh, Teresa?"

Patiently Mother Paganini set to work, making smaller the great coat of her husband. But as she slipped the heavy garment over the thin little shoulders, her soft dark eyes were troubled.

"Could we not wait a little longer, Toni?" she questioned anxiously. "The child is so young to begin to earn a living."

"Young? Come now, Teresa, a little work can do him no harm. But it's time the boy was off. And you, Lucca," he added, "see that you scamper lively after the coins!"

His first adventure! Nicolo stood in the market square, his bright red coat buttoned high under his chin. Nimbly his bow skipped over the strings of his small violin as a crowd gathered quickly.

"How well he plays for such a little mite! Ah yes, but how hungry he looks. Bravo! More! More!" echoed on all sides.

On to the tavern went the pair. But now, poor Nicolo could scarcely play, with the odor of roasting meats making him hungrier than ever.

"Could we take a few coins and go inside, Lucca?" he whispered. "Then you will see how I will play, and we will have more coins than ever."

In a moment the boys were in the tavern, eating a plateful of steaming sausages such as they had never seen in all their lives.

"Young man," a voice broke in on the feasting, "when you have finished, I would like to hear you play again."

The waiter shuffled to the table as the tall stranger left. "Better be good, boy, or the leader of the orchestra will know it."

The leader of the orchestra! Nicolo wiped the juice from his lips, his eyes round. "He plays the violin, too?" he questioned.

"None better," was the reply. "Known all over these parts."

A warm glow stole over him as Nicolo left his chair to tune his small instrument. If only there were sausages every day, he could play for the whole world and never grow weary.

The laughter and loud talking were stilled as the melody began, the pure tones melting together in loveliest sound. With a sigh, the song was ended, and the tall man was beside him again.

"Bring your father to the theater tomorrow afternoon," said he, briskly. "Be on time, at three. I am a very busy man."

He was gone, and the waiter was chuckling as he shook bright coins in the palm of his bony hand.

"Lire he gave me for your sausages! A good start for the day, eh?"

Such excitement as there was in the Paganini home that evening!

"Our luck is changing, Teresa!" exclaimed Antonio. "To think of our Nico playing for a director! Like Mozart it sounds already!"

The next afternoon Nicolo stood with his father before Signor Servetto, his violin safe in the green flannel bag under his arm.

"The boy has a good tone, sir." The director spoke rapidly as he twirled the ends of his light moustache. "I would like to teach him to play well, if you are willing."

Antonio could scarcely believe his ears. But the next moment, an anxious frown crossed his brow.

"I – I am a very poor man, sir," he began. "The lessons–"

"No need for worry," the leader answered quickly. "Some day the boy may be useful here." He waved his hand toward the pit where the musicians were taking their places for a rehearsal. "And remember," the director spoke firmly now, "no more street playing!"

This was a blow, indeed. No coins to help buy bread! Nodding his head, Antonio turned to go.

But Nicolo was lost in the sounds. Closer and closer to the men he had crept, until he was almost in the pit with them.

The director smiled. "Let him stay. He can do no harm."

Nicolo was in the front seat now, his breath coming short and fast. Strings and horns were all singing together in such beautiful music that he wanted to laugh and weep and shout, all at once.

The rehearsal was over at last, and the director found the young listener crouched in one corner of the seat, his small white face wet with tears.

"Come tomorrow, Nico," said he gently, his hand on the slender shoulder. "You and I will have fine times together, yes?"

There was no need of calling him the next morning. With the first gray dawn, Nicolo scrambled from his pallet. It was lesson day!

Quietly he crept into the cold kitchen and, pulling hard on the pump handle, bent his head under the icy stream. He must be clean for his first lesson with the director.

Slipping into his red coat, he searched the old cupboard for a crust of bread, but not a crumb was there to be found. Down the stairs and out into the street he ran, his violin clutched in his hand. He must not keep the director waiting.

But what was this? The doors of the theater were tightly closed. Seating himself on the cold steps to wait, Nicolo watched a man at the curb pouring out grain for his hungry horse. In a moment he was beside the lean pair, his fingers outstretched toward the sack.

"Breakfast?" Chuckling, the man let the grains trickle into the small palm. "What's good for hosses is good for young 'uns, I reckon. Ought to be home in bed, though, child. Hardly sunup, yet!"

But Nicolo was back at the steps, and drawing his knees under his coat to keep warm, his small teeth ground away on the hard kernels. Pale sunrays, creeping around the edge of the building, made a little pool of light about him, and slowly the grinding ceased as a gentle drowsiness came over him. Leaning his head against the stone wall, he was soon in the land of dreams.

Suddenly a loud banging startled him almost out of his wits.

"Bless me, if it isn't the young violinist!" exclaimed the old doorkeeper. "Come in! Come in out of the dampness, child!"

Seeing the grain in the small hand, he pulled two hard yellow buns from his back pocket and, handing one to Nicolo, sat down beside him in the dim theater.

"Now I was just sayin' to my old missus that I'd best have a bite of breakfast on hand, case I got hollow in the middle," said he.

As they were finishing their small meal, footsteps sounded in the hallway, and Nicolo sprang to his feet, his heart thumping hard inside him. His first lesson with the director was at hand.

"Upon my word! Ahead of time you are, boy!" cried Signor Servetto, looking down at the eager little figure. "Off with that fine red coat, and we will get started."

The instrument was tuned so quickly that the director could scarcely believe his eyes. And every string was in perfect key.

"Good! Now we start at the beginning. Ready! Bow across the strings, slowly–slowly. Keep the violin high. Bow straight. Again!"

The leader sighed at the end of the lesson. How speedily the child learned! Never had he had a pupil like him.

"Much music there is inside you, boy," said he solemnly. "We must be sure to guide it well. Come again in two days. But wait until I have had my breakfast, please!"

Nicolo's thin little face lighted in a smile.

"Oh yes, sir!" he breathed. "Just two days and I can come again!" Skipping off to the Passage of the Black Cat, he scampered up the long stairs, happily telling the news.

"So the lesson was good." Antonio was pleased as he finished his noonday meal of bread and cheese. "But each time it must be better, Nico. Better! Do you hear? Off with you now to the practicing."

Alone in the small room, Nicolo heard the key turn in the lock behind him. He was a prisoner, indeed, and would not be free again until long hours of hard work were at an end.

Over and over the exercises he went until his short arms ached, and he longed to put the instrument down. As merry laughter floated up to him from the street below, where the children were busy with their games, faster and faster Nicolo played with all his might, to drown out the sounds.

Six long hours went by, and spent and hungry, he fell to the pallet on the floor, too weary to cry out. Darkness had fallen, and from the shadows a flickering candle came slowly toward him.

"Nico, little Nico!" His mother was bending over him, stroking his arms with her work-hardened hands. "It is enough now, small one. See what I have brought you!"

The hot soup of spaghetti, flavored with vegetables, smelled good to Nicolo. Cooling it a little, Teresa's heart ached as she watched the delicate brooding face, stained with tears.

"A secret I have to tell you, my Nico," she comforted, spooning the broth into the small mouth. "In the darkness of night, the most wonderful dream came to me. A shining angel stood by my bed, making the room brighter than day."

Nicolo's tired eyes began to open a little, and he pushed away the soup. "Tell me more." His words were like a sigh.

"Then the angel began to speak," went on his mother. "Slowly and clearly her words came to me. 'Your son will be a famous musician some day,' said she. 'Even more–he will become the greatest violinist in all the world.' And then the light faded and the angel was gone."

For two years the practicing and the lessons went on. And many times, when he thought he could go on no longer, his mother would say in her gentle way, "Remember the angel, Nico. Great things she promised for you!"

Always the words brought new life and courage. And when he was just eight, Nicolo played so well that the director of the orchestra spoke earnestly with Antonio one day.

"Your son has learned all that I have to teach him," said he. "Now he must have a new master. Why not try Giacomo Costa, the finest violinist in all Genoa? He would do much for the boy."

As they started homeward, Antonio laughed happily. "Soon you may play as well as the boy Mozart!" he cried. "And then we can live in better quarters. Why, we might even have a fine carriage, like the one coming toward us!"

The proud horses in harness of shining silver, pranced by, and Nicolo looked with awe at the nobleman and fair lady in rich costumes of velvet and fine lace, chatting together pleasantly as they rode along. But such a life would never be for him.

That very afternoon he hurried to the Cathedral with his father, to be greeted by the plump Signor Costa, a smile on his round face.

"The Paganinis!" he beamed. "And a good report of you has just come to me, boy. Play for me now, and we will see what needs to be done."

Nicolo felt strangely at peace in the presence of the kindly master. The tones of his violin took on warmth and beauty as joyously he played the last composition that he had just learned.

The director sat up in astonishment. Here was rare talent, indeed! Quietly he placed his hand on Nicolo's shaggy head.

"The boy will study with me, Signor Paganini. And I hope that I shall be worthy of the trust placed in me."

"What luck is ours today, eh Nico?" cried Antonio as they went out into the street. "To celebrate, the rest of the afternoon is yours."

Free hours of his own! Off raced Nicolo like an arrow—straight to the docks and his good friend of the sea.

"Nico! I thought you had forgotten old Romano!" With gnarled hands the old man divided his fish cake with his young visitor. "Bright tadpoles!" he went on. "So fine you are in the red coat that I can hardly see you under it!" He peered into the shining young face and smiled.

"It's to help me to be another Mozart," explained Nicolo quickly. "And Romano," his voice sank to a whisper, "the angel came out of the heavens, and she said I would be a great violinist some day!"

Romano chewed in silence, and then the little blue tassel on his cap was very busy.

"Now for my part," said he, briskly, "I'd rather you'd stay just plain Nicolo. And besides, I was countin' on your comin' down to give me a hand with the nets, come another few years."

Looking out longingly over the blue waters, Nicolo's voice was small and wistful.

"But Romano, could we catch enough fish so that we could live in beautiful houses and ride around in fine carriages?"

The little blue tassel was quiet now. "Why no, Nico, I reckon not quite that many fish. Better stay with the fiddle, boy."

It was time for the old fisherman to get on with his chores, and off ran Nicolo to explore the busy waterfront. What fun it was to take a short ride out to sea on the choppy waters and then to watch the loading of the ships along the wharf, creeping aboard like a shadow now and then, to enjoy a tasty bite with the cook in the warm galley.

When the moon had stretched long silver fingers across the water, he sighed happily and found his way home, stumbling to his pallet on the hard floor and rolling himself into a little ball to try to keep warm for the night.

The next morning, Signor Costa listened in wonder to his youngest pupil. How fast his bow raced over the strings in the most difficult music! What a joy to teach this boy from the poorest part of Genoa!

But as the weeks went on, and the winter rainstorms lashed the old city walls, he looked with dismay at the tired, sad-faced student, with little body so thin that a gust of wind could blow it away. If only there was a way to stop the look of hunger in the wistful eyes.

"A little surprise today, Nico," he would say before the lesson began. From behind his back he would bring warm crusty bread, or nuts and dried fruit, and not until the last crumb had disappeared, did the work begin.

One morning, the director smiled at the end of the hard lesson.

"You are ready now, my child," said he quietly. "You will play this solo in the services at the Cathedral on Sunday morning."

Home through the rainstorm darted Nicolo, shouting his good news. "Mother! Father! You will be happy now. I play a composition in the church!"

Antonio could scarcely contain himself for joy. His heavy sandals flapped against the rough cobbles as he ran to spread the word among the neighbors.

"Already our Nico is famous! He plays a fine solo in the Cathedral. Come to the church and see for yourself!"

Sunday morning dawned clear and brisk, and never was a father prouder than Antonio, as he took his place with his family and neighbors in the quiet Cathedral. At once he pointed to Nicolo, whose head just showed above the railing, high in the loft.

With solemn chords the organ began to play, and his small violin tucked under his chin, Nicolo drew the bow slowly over the strings.

The people looked up in astonishment. A mite of a child was bringing them music from another world. Antonio sat on the edge of his chair, breathing heavily, and when the last beautiful note was stilled, he leaned toward Teresa, nudging her arm.

"No sick notes, eh, wife?" His whispered words echoed around him.

The next morning the director looked long at his young pupil. He must be careful not to spoil him with too much praise.

"Yes, the playing was good, Nicolo." He nodded his gray head as he spoke. "But more lessons there must be, especially in composition, with so much melody in your small head that must come out."

Nicolo studied the floor, his cheeks flushed.

"Ah yes, I know, child. But now you might like to help pay for the lessons," said the master kindly. "Hm, let me see–" he studied the black book on the table. "Yes, here is a festival where a violinist is needed, and a wedding, just two days away. Do you think you could be ready?"

Nicolo's dark eyes glowed happily. "Oh yes, sir, I could play for the whole city!" he cried. The next minute, such a jolly melody danced from the strings that the director sprang from his chair to march gaily around the room.

"Child! Child!" he laughed and applauded merrily. "Where did the tune come from?"

"Why–it just ran into my head, and out again on the strings!"

The director smiled and pointed a warning finger. "Remember, Nico, –more lessons in writing music ! We will speak to Gnecco at once."

It was fun to set down the tunes that came so easily into his mind, but making them into compositions was quite another matter. One morning, he startled his strict new teacher by putting a difficult work on the clavier before him.

"Variations on a Theme, by Nicolo Paganini," read the master, Gnecco. "Well! Well! Let us try this fine-looking composition, young man."

He had not gone far with the clavier part when he stopped suddenly. "This is something that the others must hear," he declared. Striding to the door, he called, "Santo! Bring everyone, at once!"

Soon masters and students were gathered around, listening closely as Nicolo began the melody on his violin. Simply it started, then grew more difficult as the same melody was played in many different ways, –now sad, now merry, and ending in a spirited march.

"Good! Bravo! Nico!" rang on all sides.

Gnecco listened to the praises showered on his young pupil and rose quickly from the clavier.

"A good start," said he. "Now you may go on with your composition, and next week, bring me eight new variations on the same melody."

Eight variations! Never would there be time enough to work them out, unless he labored far into the night. And so every evening, after the family was in bed, Nicolo sat alone in the cold kitchen, setting down pages of notes through the long hours. But well repaid he was by the look of pride in the eyes of his teacher as he listened to the new work.

And more festivals there were, now, where he could play, and Nicolo was happy, indeed, to be earning a little money to help pay for his lessons.

Late one afternoon he sauntered home through the darkening streets, well pleased with his day's work. The wedding at the big house had gone well, and bright coins jingled merrily in his pocket.

And my, how he had feasted on nuts and cakes!

Smiling happily, he climbed the steps and stood near his door. But how quiet it was! Where could everyone be? Entering softly, he was startled at the sight of a stranger talking to his father. Teresa and the children stood near the small kitchen, listening with all their ears.

"Here is the boy now, Signor," declared Antonio. "Come, Nico, the gentleman has brought us good news!"

But the stranger was forgotten as the children rushed around their brother, all talking at the same time.

"You will play in a big hall, Nico! With two singers you will play. And you must have fine clothes to wear!"

Quietly the stranger left, and Antonio and Teresa could not get their words out fast enough in finishing the story.

"The biggest time of our lives, Nico! To think of your playing in the largest concert hall! And noble families from all over the country will be there to hear you!"

Nicolo was dazed by the words that rang in his ears. His first concert in the city of Genoa! Secretly he had been at work composing variations on a French martial song, loved by all the people. If only he could finish it in time for the great concert, just three short weeks away!

CHAPTER TWO

It was just an hour until concert time, and the little Paganini home was bursting with excited neighbors as Nicolo donned his fine new clothes.

"Rich black velvet they are! And real lace ruffles on the white silk blouse!" they whispered in awe.

There, ready at last. With a cry of delight, Nicolo spun around on his heels, bowing in every direction.

"Careful, Nico! Careful!" warned his mother. "Do not bend too far from the waist, or the stitches will give way!"

Quickly straightening himself after dusting the shining buckles of his new shoes, Nicolo's white teeth showed in a wide smile.

"I hardly know myself!" he exclaimed, running his fingers over the soft material. "I wish I could wear the costume every day!"

His family and the neighbors stood in an admiring circle, their cries echoing on all sides.

"There'll be no finer costume in the hall tonight! Just see the cut of him! Every inch a young nobleman he looks."

It was time to go, and the little family hurried off into the night. Arriving at the big stone building, Nicolo made his way behind the scenes. Peeking through a crack in the curtain, his eyes grew wider by the minute as royal ladies and gentlemen swept to their velvet-lined boxes. Brocades and satins whispered over the carpets, and rare jewels glowed under the brilliant lights. My, what a sight it was!

At last the hall was quiet, and the noted singer, Marchese, came to the platform in a round of applause. His beautiful voice rang through the room as he sang for the fine audience, and Nicolo watched in awe as he swept backstage.

Soon a loud knock sounded for attention, and in the hush that followed, Nicolo walked quietly to the front of the platform and bowed low as his master had taught him.

Cries of astonishment echoed in the crowded hall.

"But he is only a child! And to be placed on the program with two such famous singers? Surely there has been some mistake!"

But the next moment, such glory poured from the strings of the small violin that the people sat up, amazed. A boy of nine, and playing a work of his own! It was almost too much to believe.

Without a sign of fear, Nicolo played on. One lovely variation after another from his martial "La Carmagnole" danced along, until the audience was swaying and tapping to the spirited music.

"Bravo! Bravo!" the cries rang out even before the composition was ended. Bowing many times, Nicolo left the stage. But the people would not let him go, and their calling and clapping did not stop until he played the stirring music over again, from beginning to end.

Antonio hurried behind the scenes, watching proudly as members of the audience came to shake the hand of the young artist.

"A beautiful concert! You must play for us again, and soon, young man," they cried.

All the way home through the darkened streets, Nicolo skipped excitedly, happy with his evening's adventure.

"If only I could play every night!" he cried as the little family climbed the steps to their poor dwelling.

At his words, Antonio spun around as a thought came to him.

"Why shouldn't our Nico give a concert of his own and ask the two singers to perform with him?" he asked the startled group.

"The very thing!" cried Nicolo in delight. "And we will invite everyone in Genoa to come!"

The very next morning Antonio set to work, and soon every billboard in the city was covered with posters:

GRAND CONCERT BY NICOLO PAGANINI

BOY WONDER OF THE STRINGS

AIDED BY TWO SINGERS

And what a success the concert turned out to be! A larger crowd than ever hurried to the hall, where Nicolo played again his "Carmagnole Variations" for the cheering audience.

For days now, everyone spoke of the boy violinist, and the name of Nicolo Paganini was known through all of Genoa.

"So, my child, –the praise has not left its mark on you." The master looked searchingly into the face of his pupil who stood before him in old ragged clothing. "It is good," he declared. "Now then, every Sunday you will play an entire concerto in the church service. No lazy fingers from nothing to do, eh boy?"

"No–no, sir." Nicolo's answer was like a sigh. A long and difficult composition to be learned by heart each week!

The months followed one another swiftly, and every Sunday the crowds grew ever larger as the people hurried to the Cathedral to hear a glorious concerto played by the boy violinist.

One morning, as the difficult melodies flowed through the dim church, Antonio listened carefully and slowly shook his head. Yes, the boy had outgrown the masters, Costa and Gnecco. He must have a new teacher. Signor Rolla, famous conductor and violinist and composer, would be the man. But he lived in the city of Parma, some distance away, and funds would be needed for such a journey and much more for lessons, besides.

Here was a problem, indeed. But on the way home, a plan came to him suddenly.

"Nico, we will give another concert," he declared. "And on the billboards we will say:

GRAND PAGANINI CONCERT
FUNDS NEEDED FOR STUDY
COME ONE, COME ALL
HELP THE WONDER VIOLINIST TO GREATER FAME."

"But Father," Nicolo's voice was small in his throat, "what if the master, Rolla, will not take me for his pupil?"

Antonio's laughter brushed away the very thought. "Take you, child? Why, no one would refuse the son of Antonio Paganini!"

The concert brought greater funds than he had dreamed, and in delight, Antonio counted the pile before him the next morning.

"We are ready!" he cried. "Call the carriage, Teresa!"

Carefully tying the banknotes in a stout leathern sack, he climbed into the coach beside Nicolo.

"To Parma!" he called to the old driver, and with noisy clatter they were off.

Over the brown countryside they journeyed and, after

long hours, arrived at the door of the famous master with screeching brakes. His heart beating fast, Nicolo followed the servant to a small dark room and sat on the edge of a chair to wait.

Soon, light footsteps sounded on the stone floor, and kindly Signora Rolla entered, her head done up in a bright blue shawl.

"I am sorry to tell you, but the master is very ill and can see no one," she explained in low tones. But after a look at her young visitor, she added quickly, "One moment, and I will speak to him."

The long journey in vain? Surely it could not be!

Suddenly Antonio's eyes lighted on a new composition of the master, the pages black with notes. How difficult it would be, even to attempt to perform!

"Quickly, Nico!" he whispered. "Play the music! It is our only chance."

In a moment, the master's violin was in his hands, and the difficult composition was ringing through the house, Nicolo nodding for his father to turn the pages. When the last note was ended, a rasping voice came from the next room.

"Who plays my music?"

"Only a child, sir," Antonio answered at once.

"Impossible! Come here at once and let me see!"

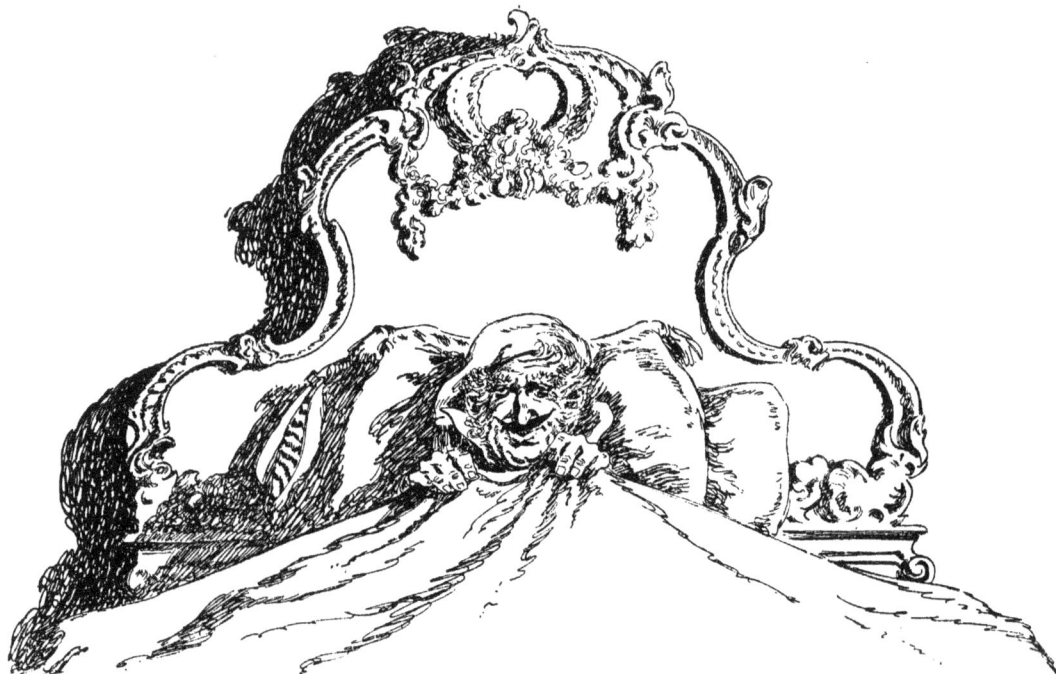

Nicolo and Antonio walked quietly through the doorway to find the master, his cheeks flushed, raised on his elbows in the bed.

"So!" he gasped. "Then it is true. A miracle, –yes, sir, a miracle!"

His sickness was forgotten as he lifted his eyes to Antonio's smiling face. "See here, my good man, I can teach your son nothing. But lessons in composition he must have, plenty of them."

Settling himself back in the bed, he drew the covers around his neck, fastening his eyes on Nicolo.

"Heavenly angels! I never would have believed it–never!" he breathed. Suddenly he sat bolt upright, shaking his finger. "See that you come back here tomorrow, boy! A secret I have to give you."

The next morning, there was the great Rolla in bright red dressing gown seated in a chair, the servants rushing about to make him comfortable.

"Good thing you are here, boy, or all these heads would be rolling from their shoulders!" he barked, his nightcap bobbing angrily. "Come, come, child–hand me the fiddle," he commanded.

His fingers trembling a little, Nicolo tuned it quickly.

"Now then, many secrets there are in playing. Watch, boy. Strike the strings so hard with the bow that it will bounce back quickly. Try it now. Harder! Faster. There, see what a shower of bright tones leap from the instrument, all at once!"

Nicolo was delighted with the many new ways of playing and spent long hours in practicing what he had learned. Each morning, when he returned to the hard taskmaster, Rolla laughed with glee.

"Work, boy, –work is what does it, eh?" he would growl. "And thinking carefully as you practice. You will show them all one day how the violin can speak to the hearts of men as no other instrument."

And now, long lessons there were with the great master, Ghiretti, in learning how to write for instruments of the orchestra.

"But I would like the music to be harder," declared the young student, frowning over the fugues that he was composing.

The master laughed and rapped his pupil smartly on the back. "Why so difficult, small one? No one will be able to perform them."

Nicolo looked up with a mischievous smile. "Then I will play them all myself!" he answered.

At the end of six months of hard work, the twenty-four wonderful fugues were finished, and Ghiretti shook his head in amazement. Never before had anyone accomplished so difficult a task.

"Well done, my pupil!" he exclaimed. "I hope that I may be in the audience someday when you play this fine composition."

Back to Genoa went Nicolo with his father, well content with what he had learned in the old city of Parma.

"One thing before us now, my son," Antonio was planning again. "When you have learned enough music for many programs, we will start on a concert tour, like the boy, Mozart."

A concert tour! Nicolo breathed faster as he took bites of the cold fish lying in a cracked dish on the rickety table.

His father went on, jubilantly. "Then houses and lands and carriages will be ours for the asking, when we return home again."

"And real beds to sleep in, with covers," added Nicolo. "And we will never be hungry again."

There must be plenty of compositions of his own, and now he could make them as difficult as he liked. Nicolo smiled as he set to work. And so hard were the works that carne from his pen, that ten long hours he practiced on a single page, before he was able to play it.

At last, after two long years, it was time to set out. Bundles were carefully stored in the coach, and all was ready. My, what excitement there was as Teresa and the children and neighbors fluttered around with last minute offerings!

"Wear it for luck whenever you play," Shoemaker Paolo thrust a squirrel's foot into Nicolo's hand. "And this little bottle of herbs, Nico—a little in the shoes will keep the evil

spirits away. Be sure to wrap up well after the concerts and mind your manners at the homes of noblemen. Good-bye! Good-bye!"

One morning, not far from the town where the first concert was to be given, a light rain began to fall, and soon the roads were churned into thick red mud. Slipping and sliding, the coach jolted this way and that, and uneasily Antonio called out to the driver.

"Better put up at the side of the road until the storm is over, or we'll be at the bottom of the ditch!"

The old man clung to the reins, shouting back his answer.

"Too narrow here for passing, sir. We'll try it around the bend."

Cautiously they rounded the sharp turn, when suddenly one of the horses slipped and fell, bringing the second down with him. In an instant the carriage was rolling down the steep bank–down, down to the bottom of the gully.

"Nico! Nico! Are you hurt, boy?" Antonio shouted, his face white as he looked at the still figure on the floor.

Carefully they carried him to the mail coach and drove slowly into town, where he was hastily put to bed at the inn.

Outside the door an anxious group of town folk made way for the doctor.

"It's the Boy Wonder of the Violin. Bad accident on the roadway. No playing tomorrow night, and perhaps never again."

In low tones the doctor spoke to Antonio. "A narrow escape, my good man. He will awaken soon but must be kept quiet for several days."

At last Nicolo was able to be up and about, and the next week, two concerts had to be given, so that all might see and hear the wonder violinist. In hushed silence the people listened, enraptured, to the thirteen-year-old artist. Then their cries and applause rang on and on, to be stilled only when Nicolo returned to play again.

"He is rightly called the Boy Wonder of the Strings!" they declared.

To concert halls, palaces, and fine homes of noblemen went Nicolo, astonishing all who heard him.

"Bravo! Bravo, Paganini!" sounded in his ears night after night as he held his faithful violin under his chin, playing as no other boy violinist had ever done before.

Gifts were showered on him, and nodding wisely, Antonio carefully wrapped the precious articles for safe keeping.

"Presents are all very fine and will come in handy some day. But it is golden coins we need, eh Nico?" he would say.

After long weeks of playing in beautiful Lombardy, the concerts came to an end, and off started the travelers for home. At last, one bright morning, as they drove into the Passage of the Black Cat with rousing clatter, delighted cries rang up and down the street to welcome them.

"They're home! The Paganinis have just arrived!"

With a grand flourish, Antonio spread out the gifts before the awed neighbors, telling for hours how they were bestowed on the gallant young violinist in the finest homes in all the land.

"And now we are rich, Father!" cried the children. "Houses and lands and carriages and beds we will have!"

A frown darkened Antonio's brow. "Not everything can come at once," he answered slowly. "A little at a time is the best way."

As the months rolled by and Nicolo went on working at his music, a secret longing grew within him, a longing to be out in the world again. He must find a way to go, and this time, he must go alone.

Quietly he began to plan. To Paolo he took himself one afternoon at sunset, just as the little cobbler was taking off his apron.

"Ah, the Genius of the Strings! What can I do for you, neighbor?"

Nicolo held up his foot. "See, Paolo, new shoes I must have. These cannot be soled again, and too short they are, besides."

"Growing, always growing *up*, you are, Nico. But never out *sideways*!" laughed Paolo at his little joke. "But look you, boy, how will the fine new shoes be paid for?" he asked quietly.

Slowly Nicolo unfolded his plan. "I thought–perhaps I could teach your children how to play on the fiddle or the mandolin. Often they have asked me, but there has never been time." His voice became anxious now. "I would teach them well, Paolo, and play for them, oh, many times, besides."

The toothless cobbler stroked his chin thoughtfully.

"Not a bad bargain," he agreed slowly. "Not at all a bad bargain."

Nicolo's heart leaped for joy when the shoes and the lessons were begun at the same time. His little plan was working! But his next errand would be more difficult, much more difficult, he said to himself as he went down the street to call on the tailor.

"A new suit!" exclaimed Signor Angelo, looking at the tall boy with arms dangling from his coat sleeves. Here was a problem, indeed.

"Except for my concert costume, they would be the first new clothes in my life, sir. Always my father's or the neighbors' coats have been cut down for me." Nicolo's words tumbled one onto another.

The tailor looked long at the ragged, delicate figure. What suffering there had been, with barely enough food to keep the young life going. His voice was kind as he went on with his questioning.

"But cloth is very dear, to say nothing of the long hours of labor. Who would pay for it all, boy?"

Nicolo took a deep breath and answered bravely. "I thought, sir, that you might like to invite all your friends to a grand festival."

"So!" exclaimed Angelo, laughing. "And you would play for the dancing?"

"Oh yes, but I would do much more, sir," replied Nicolo, his eyes growing darker as he went on with his plan. "I would give a whole concert beforehand, with such music as you never heard before!"

His voice was wistful now. "Oh sir, you would like the special evening, I am sure!" he exclaimed, his hands clasped tightly together.

Suddenly the tailor put his arm around the thin shoulders.

"Agreed, Nicolo! You will plan the music, while I plan the clothes!"

Nicolo brushed away the tears of joy as he sped on winged feet to the market square. Up the stairs he ran, and beneath a great golden fiddle swinging over the door, he found his friend Ricci, famous maker and mender of violins.

"New strings today?" greeted the gentle little man, his shoulders bowed with long years of work.

"No, master. My fiddle has a crack that needs mending."

With delicate fingers, Ricci carefully examined the opening.

"Ah yes. Two days it will take. But I will lend you a violin for the practicing."

Quietly Nicolo went about the shop, lightly plucking the

strings of each of the instruments hanging on the walls.

"Only listen, Ricci!" he exclaimed. "Each violin has its own way of speaking, –gentle or harsh or sad."

The little workman smiled and, holding up a finger, disappeared into the back of the shop. Soon he was back, a long velvet case in his hands. Without a word he unlocked it and drew from it gently, an instrument that quivered at his touch.

"You will not soon forget this day, Nicolo," said he in hushed tones. "Before you is one of the greatest treasures of the world, brought to me for safekeeping in the vault."

The young boys who were learning how to make violins,

crept close to the table, never taking their eyes from the famous instrument.

"It must be played on, now and then," went on Ricci, softly. "And today, that privilege shall be yours."

A Stradivarius violin! Nicolo could scarcely believe his eyes. Taking a deep breath, he lifted the rare instrument to his shoulder and drew the bow gently over the strings. A cry of joy came from his lips as the light free tone poured from the glorious treasure.

"Oh, Master Ricci!" he exclaimed, quickly handing back the violin. "I do not dare to play on it longer. I would never be content with my poor little fiddle again!"

"Pure tone, eh Nico?" sighed the workman, as carefully he wrapped the instrument in its silken coverings. "It is worth more than you or I will ever know in this lifetime. The old master who made it knew his secrets well. To no one did he pass them on, so that now, the rare instruments that came from his hands are treasured by kings or noblemen and placed in glass cases for safe keeping."

For days, as Nicolo went about his work, he could think of nothing but the sound of the noble Stradivarius violin. If

only some day he might have a fine instrument, how he would play!

But now, there was his promise to be kept, and faithfully Nicolo taught the children of Paolo to play on the mandolin and the guitar. How pleased he was when they performed by heart little pieces for their proud father!

"An excellent teacher you have proven yourself to be," cried the delighted shoemaker. "And you shall have your reward. Soon the shoes will be finished, and well you have earned them, young man."

Two fittings there had been at the tailor's, and little shivers ran up and down Nicolo's back at the thought that, before long, all would be in readiness for the special journey. All but the most difficult thing: speaking to Antonio of his plans.

One morning, after his breakfast of bread, he swallowed hard and turned to his father.

"I would like to go to the festival at Lucca and play for the people on St. Martin's Day," said he, his voice sounding very small.

Antonio looked up, startled.

"The neighbors have been speaking of the festival, Nico. But I had not thought of making the journey." He paused a moment and then nodded slowly. "But there is no reason why we could not go."

Nicolo breathed quickly and his words tumbled out.

"This time I would like to go alone, Father. I am old enough now to care for myself."

Antonio pushed himself from the table, rising quickly.

"If I do not go with you, then your older brother must accompany you," he decided shortly.

Nicolo, surprised at his own courage, spoke more steadily now.

"No, Father. I will go alone to Lucca."

There was no answer as Antonio strode away, his footsteps echoing down the long stairs as he went on his way to the wharf to load foodstuffs on the low, flat barges.

Nicolo was never so joyous, his whole life long. In just two short days he would be ready to leave, to seek his fortune in the wide world, alone.

CHAPTER THREE

Nicolo raised himself from his pallet and listened carefully in the darkness of early morning. It must be earlier than he thought, with no sounds but the signal horns in the harbor and the heavy breathing of his father in the room just beyond.

Slipping quietly into the new suit and shining black shoes, he started softly down the long stairs. Creak! Creak! The new leather spoke too loudly, and in a moment the shoes were carried swiftly to the street.

The Passage of the Black Cat was strangely quiet under the November stars as Nicolo took a last look at the tumbledown place where he had spent all of his years.

Queer feelings came over him as he strode rapidly away, his footsteps echoing sharply on the hard cobbles.

He was free at last, —free! free! free! He wanted to shout the words to the fresh new morning. Faster and faster his long thin legs ate up the ground toward Lucca, joyous whistling piping from his lips.

What did it matter if there was not a single coin in his pocket for food or lodging? His trusty fiddle would see to that for him! Settling his violin more comfortably in the hollow of his arm, a bright smile spread over his face as he raised his eyes to the paling heavens over his head.

Turning up his coat collar against the raw wind, Nicolo felt a gnawing hunger growing inside him. But no sign of an inn was there, and he hastened his steps to forget the hollow emptiness.

Three miles were well behind him when he spied a small farmhouse beside the road. A curl of gray smoke told of a fire on the hearth, and in a few moments, Nicolo was at the door.

"I am on my way to Lucca and would be glad of a bite of breakfast, sir," said he.

The poor fanner looked closely at the traveler through the narrow opening. "You wouldn't be askin' if you couldn't pay, I reckon?"

"Oh no, sir," answered Nicolo quickly, slipping inside. How glad he was to warm himself at the fire with the flock of ragged children!

At one end of the wide hearth stood their mother, her head wrapped in a piece of old linen, as briskly she stirred the pot of

bubbling porridge. Soon Nicolo was sharing the simple meal, and never did anything taste so good.

When the last spoonful had disappeared, he quietly drew his violin from the green flannel bag, and a jolly country tune rollicked through the tiny cottage, bringing the children in a laughing, dancing ring around him. Then closer and closer they pressed as a new kind of music sang to them, –a plaintive, lonely melody of far-open stretches of sea.

The farmer and his wife stood flattened against the wall, their eyes as large as the children's as they listened to such music as they had never dreamed of before.

"Bless you, boy." murmured the peasant, when the melodies came to an end. Putting a freshly-baked loaf of bread and a bit of cheese into his hands, he added, "Won't come amiss on a day like this, I reckon."

Inns there were aplenty from there on, where Nicolo played for meals and a place to lay his head for the night.

At last, one fair morning, he found himself in the old city of Lucca. And what a merry sight met his eyes! In the gaily decorated streets, young folk in bright costumes were dancing to the music of little bands, drawn around on donkey carts.

"Join us! Join us!" Laughing voices sounded in his ears. The next instant, a lion's head was thrown over him, and Nicolo found himself leaping merrily about in the swirling throng. Dancing and shouting happily, he scrambled for nuts and sweetmeats with the crowd.

Suddenly church bells announced the evening, and freeing himself of the animal's head, Nicolo sighed with delight. For the first time in his life, there had been hours for fun.

Quietly he made his way to the concert hall. His coat well brushed from the dust of the roadway, he stood behind the stage, ready to play for the people of Lucca. But now a strange fear seized him. In this first concert that he, himself, had arranged by a simple letter, would there be anyone there to hear him?

Clutching his violin, he stepped to the platform, and a tumult of applause greeted him. The hall was filled to overflowing with visitors from far and near, eager to hear the Boy Wonder of the Strings.

And well did he live up to the name, holding his audience spellbound through the hours.

The concert was a success! His heart singing for joy, Nicolo sped through the dark streets to a simple inn, his pockets stuffed with crisp new banknotes. With trembling fingers, he laid them on the table before him, dividing them equally into two parts. One he would send to his father, keeping the other for himself.

Banknotes to spend as he wished! Why, he would soon be a rich man, walking about with a gold-headed cane. Leaving his chair, Nicolo bowed in lordly manner to imaginary royal friends. Then, in a fit of laughter, he threw himself on the bed and, exhausted, fell into deep slumber.

The next morning, eager for adventure, he hurried below

to enjoy a good hot breakfast, when a thought slipped into his mind. Why not go on to Pisa and to other cities and play for the people?

The plans were speedily made, and everywhere eager citizens hurried through the streets to hear the Boy Wonder.

"Long live Paganini, master of strings!" their praises echoed.

With a trusted messenger, Nicolo sent half of his earnings to Antonio. And then what good times he had! Ordering the best carriages, he traveled about in fine style and enjoyed the choicest foods and wines to be found.

"Come, comrades!" he would cry. "Join in the feasting!"

But alas for poor Nicolo! Unused to rich food, he awoke one morning very ill, indeed.

"This young man is far from strong," said the doctor to the worried innkeeper. "He must stay in bed for some time to come."

At last, when he was allowed to sit up, Nicolo called for paper and a stout pen.

"Quickly, Quickly, before the tune leaves me!" he cried.

In a rush, the notes went down in a lovely singing melody.

And by the time he was on his feet again, a fine new Caprice was ready for the audiences.

For three long years Nicolo roamed about, playing concerts and being ill in turn, until at last his thoughts turned to Genoa.

"I must go home—at once!" he announced one morning. With all haste he made a little bundle of his few possessions and started on his way.

The miles seemed never to end, so poor were the roads. But one afternoon just at sunset, Nicolo found himself rumbling over the cobbles of the Passage of the Black Cat. Leaping to the ground, his heart pounded happily as he raced up the long flights of stairs.

Teresa, busy with the evening meal, let the pot boil over as she heard the familiar footsteps.

"Nico!" she cried, rushing to meet him, her tears falling fast. "You are home at last! How long we have waited for your coming!"

"Nico! Nico!" Antonio and the neighbors were calling his name as they rushed in to welcome the wandering musician. But at sight of him, they stopped suddenly. What a man of the world he had become!

Soon the small quarters were filled to overflowing, and the celebrations began, lasting well into the night, with dancing and singing and story-telling.

And now, long months of hard work passed by, but when the warm winds began to blow in from the sea, Nicolo became ever more restless. One fine morning, taking his violin from its peg on the wall, he sauntered to his good friend, Ricci, in the square.

"It is the old crack again, master, that must be fixed before I can leave Genoa."

Signor Ricci picked up the instrument, only to put it down again swiftly.

"Nico! Perhaps there is no need of the repair. Word has just come of a rare contest in Parma. Pasini, a painter, has written a composition so difficult that no one has been able to play it. He declares that whoever masters it at sight, shall have as a reward, one of the treasures of his life—a Stradivarius violin."

Nicolo breathed deeply, and a long sigh came from his lips.

"All my life I have dreamed of owning a fine instrument. But a rare Stradivarius! Ah no, it was never meant for me, Ricci."

A frown darkened the brow of the little violin maker.

"Come, Nico! What harm would there be in trying the composition?"

Rousing himself from his thoughts, Nicolo looked into the warm brown eyes.

"Very well, my friend. For you, alone, I will enter the contest."

His earnings spent, there was nothing to do but walk the hundred long miles to the home of the painter, and soon Nicolo was on the road leading to Parma.

On the third day, his poor feet were hot and blistering, and stopping by the roadway, he dabbled them in a small, icy stream. Ah, how good it felt! Refreshed, he reached for his violin, and the loveliest melody filled the sunlit air.

Suddenly, a sharp noise behind him startled him, and turning quickly, he discovered a young man beaming at him from a green bush.

"I only meant to listen a moment and go on my way, when the stick broke under my foot," explained the stranger hastily. "My name is Germi, and I am on my way to Parma, to finish my studies there."

"Parma!" echoed Nicolo. "My destination, as well. I am Paganini."

A low whistle was Germi's reply. "The violinist from Genoa, where I was born!" he exclaimed. "Perhaps we could go on together, unless you are traveling by coach."

Nicolo laughed shortly. "My way is the same as yours. And it might be well to cover a few miles before sundown."

Soon the boys were on their way, talking together happily of their plans for the future.

"See here, Nico!" said fair-haired Germi suddenly. "You need a good manager for your concerts. Now who would be better suited than I, with my training for a lawyer?" His blue eyes became serious. "No more worries for you—no more figuring..."

"No more figuring!" broke in Nicolo. "Do you know, my friend, that you travel the highway with a man who can count only on his fingers? It's true. You see, Germi, never a day have I spent in a schoolroom. While my brother and two sisters went, I was obliged to spend the hours at home, in practicing."

Germi listened quietly and then a merry smile lighted his face. "All the more reason why I should help you with your affairs. Your hand on the bargain, Nico! Lucky you are to have found an honest partner!"

The two laughed together at the strange new pact. But the next moment they were busy with planning.

"We could start with a first concert in Parma," said Nicolo, eagerly. "And plenty there will be for you to do, my fine manager. Notices must be made and posted round the town, tickets printed, a hall rented, and an accompanist to be found." He stopped short in the roadway. "But what will we do for money for all of these things?"

This was a thought, indeed. But the new manager was not to be daunted. Pulling out his beautiful watch, he twirled it on golden chain.

"This, my dear Nicolo Paganini, and a few banknotes, besides."

How good it was to have a companion, thought Nicolo. All his life he had longed for someone who could share his troubles. Happier than he had been in many long years, he entered the city of Parma, where the two parted company.

Not a word of the contest had he told his new friend. There would be time for that later.

Asking his way, Nicolo stood at last before the home of the painter, Pasini, his breath coming quickly. One of the rarest treasures in all the world lay just inside this house! His heart beating hard against his chest, he knocked at the door.

A servant in somber costume answered his call.

"I have come to try the master's composition, if he will allow me," said Nicolo, his voice sounding far away.

In a moment he was seated in the richly-furnished hall, listening to voices in the room just beyond.

"Another poor fiddler who cannot play better than the last, no doubt." The weary voice drifted on: "Better send him away and save me the bother."

But when the servant returned, he was startled to find a spirited young man, with eyes flashing in the dim light.

"Please tell your master that Paganini, from Genoa, is here!"

At once, a voice was raised in excited tones.

"The young violinist, Paganini? But why did you not say so? Bring him in at once!"

Master Pasini hurried to his visitor, hands outstretched. "My dear young man, forgive me! So many come who cannot even draw a bow."

Smiling, he drew Nicolo into the large workroom where the Cardinal from the cathedral was sitting for his portrait.

"Yes, yes, the violinist from Genoa," he smiled a welcome from the little platform. "And you hope to win the famous Stradivarius? The same hope has drawn musicians from all over the world, young man. And never has a rarer prize been offered."

The Cardinal raised a warning finger. "But the work of our composer, here, is no simple music! Prepare for a stout battle."

Opening a large book with pride, Pasini smiled. Here was a test for the violinist from Genoa!

"The composition must be played at sight," he explained. "And not a single error will be allowed. Will you try it now, young man?"

Nicolo tuned his violin and took a deep breath.

"I am ready, sir," he answered quietly.

With a sweep of the bow, he began, and the two men leaned forward in their chairs, listening closely to every note. On and on flowed the music, one difficult page after another. Without once stopping and with not a single mistake, Nicolo came at last to the end of the composition,

The men sprang from their chairs, crying out in amazement.

"A miracle, Paganini! You have performed a miracle!" Their exclamations rang through the room.

Signor Pasini gripped the hand of the player. "Young man, you have won the great prize!" he exclaimed. "Come—you shall see it at once."

Unlocking a glass case, the painter gently lifted two instruments from the shelf and laid them tenderly on a velvet stand.

"Precious violins are these, both made by the great master, Stradivarius," said he in hushed tones. "Now you shall make your choice."

With trembling hands, Nicolo touched his bow to the rare treasures, and the tone leaped from the strings, pure and sweet, as if by magic. Brushing the tears from his eyes with his coat sleeve, he gasped, "Forgive me, sir–it is too beautiful!" He paused a moment, and then his words rushed on, his eyes burning like coals. "Oh Signor, with this violin I will unlock the hearts of men! And they will laugh with me and weep with me. I tell you, sir, I will conquer the whole world with this instrument!"

Racing through the streets to the inn, the treasure clasped in his arms, he could not get the glorious news out fast enough. And as one in a daze, Germi listened to such playing as he had never dreamed possible. But after two hours of music, he got up quietly.

"Come, Nico—you must be weary," he begged. "Now you must have food, to be strong for our big concert, here in Parma next week."

But Nicolo did not hear and went on playing the rare instrument through the long night hours. Not until dawn did he crawl into bed, wrapping the treasure carefully in the blankets beside him.

The concert night arrived all too soon. And what a success it turned out to be! There sat the celebrated Pasini with his noble friends, listening enraptured to the music of the young violinist.

Afterward, at a fine dinner at the home of the painter, the guests crowded around Nicolo, warmly shaking his hand.

"So you are already conquering the hearts of men," said the master, smiling. "The Strad has brought you luck, I see, and well you deserve it. But guard it with your very life, young man, for there are few in all the world."

Late one afternoon Germi raced to the inn, all out of breath.

"Good news, Nico!" he cried. "We give a concert in Leghorn, with all this money in advance!"

Nicolo stared at the banknotes, piled high on the table.

"And more to come, when the tickets have been sold!" the excited manager exclaimed. "To Leghorn! We move at once!"

Soon the boys were settled in handsome quarters at the inn, and off they went to the theater to speak to the director.

"Of course the orchestra will accompany you when you play, young man," said the stocky gentleman, smoothing his silken beard.

Nicolo smiled happily. What a concert this would be!

And now, while Germi went back to his studies at Parma, Nicolo explored the lovely city of Leghorn to his heart's content and, visiting the very best tailor, ordered costly new clothing for the special occasion. There might as well be everyday coats, with a good supply of satin cravats and several pairs of the finest boots.

With so much money at hand, the days were filled with pleasures, with now and then a rehearsal with the men of the orchestra.

The afternoon of the concert arrived at last, and racing with all speed from Parma, Germi burst in upon his friend. But at sight of Nicolo's face, he stopped short.

"Nothing has gone wrong?" he cried. "You are ready to play?"

Nicolo studied the floor before answering. "I–I am ready, Germi. Only–there is no violin to play on."

The young manager could not believe his ears. "But where is the Stradivarius?" he gasped.

"Why–you see–I ordered these things," Nicolo began, his arm sweeping over the mass of new clothing. "And to pay for them, I had to borrow money on the violin."

The pain in his eyes was so great that Genni could not say the words that raced to his lips. Seizing him by the arm, he hurried him to the door.

"Quickly!" he cried. "There is not a moment to lose. Take me to the shop where you left the Strad!"

Down the street at full speed they ran, stopping at the sign of the money lender. But with all their pleading, the lean little man only shook his head.

"But we will bring you the money the moment the concert is over," cried Germi in despair. "And extra banknotes, besides."

It was in vain, and in silence the boys returned to the inn. In just one hour, the concert would begin.

"An idea!" Germi was on his feet again. "I will be back shortly, and I command you not to leave this room while I am gone."

Within a half hour he returned, a long velvet case under his arm. In an instant Nicolo pounced on it, taking from the silken coverings an instrument that gleamed in the light. Seizing the bow, he touched the strings of the beautiful violin and cried out in rapture.

"Germi! Germi! Only listen to the liquid tone! Deep and

strong and round it is. I like it even more than the Stradivarius. Oh, much more!"

Looking carefully inside, his head shot back. "A Guarnerius, Germi! A rare and precious Guarnerius! As rare as the Strad!"

Around the room he strode, playing in a frenzy of delight.

"Enough! Enough!" cried Germi. "Into your coat this minute. The audience is already seated in the hall!"

Poor Germi. At last he had Nicolo by the arm, running with him toward the theater, the dark case against his side.

"Do not let the instrument out of your sight," he commanded sternly. "Colonel Livron, the famous French collector, has loaned it to you for the concert. He will call for it, himself, when the evening is over."

A brilliant gathering there was, indeed, to hear the much-talked-of violinist. But Nicolo forgot everything about him as the rare instrument swept him to greater and greater joy, until he was playing with such power that the people arose with one accord to do him honor.

Cries of "Paganini! Master!" were still ringing in his ears hours later when tall, handsome Colonel Livron appeared backstage. His face was alight as he approached Nicolo, hand outstretched.

"I come to pay homage, young man," he exclaimed. His eyes swept to the violin. "The instrument is a fine one, eh? The best of my collection. But never could I touch it again, after your hands have played on it. If you will allow me, I should like to present it to you, with my compliments."

To be given the priceless treasure! Nicolo could only stare at the Colonel, speechless. No words came to his rescue, and grasping the collector's hand, he stumbled from the theater with Germi.

"A dream—only a dream!" he murmured.

Germi's laughter echoed through the street as he guided his friend along.

"Never did I think that I would see such poverty and riches in so short a time!" he cried.

Arriving at the inn, he stopped for a moment.

"An errand I must attend to before joining you, Nico. It will not take long," said he, disappearing into darkness.

A half hour later he was climbing the stairs, the rare Stradivarius safely under his arm. Opening the door quietly, he walked into the room. There, in the middle of the bed was Nicolo, sound asleep, his head resting against the case of the precious Guarnerius.

"Ricci!" he was muttering through half-open lips. "Miracle, Ricci!"

CHAPTER FOUR

What a morning it was in the old city of Lucca! Cannons boomed and bright banners whipped against the blue sky as excited crowds waited for a glimpse of the new princess who was coming to rule over their beloved city.

At last the cry rang up and down the gay streets.

"She comes! The Princess comes!"

What a fair sight greeted them as the procession came in view! Trumpet calls pierced the air as the band marched proudly ahead. And there were the red-coated horsemen, guarding the sister of Napoleon as she entered the gates, her shining robe gleaming with precious jewels.

Nicolo, just arrived for the festival day, watched the gold, flower-decked carriage wheel slowly by.

"Welcome, Princess Elise! Long live the Princess!" shouted the people around him.

The fame of Paganini had already reached the ears of the new ruler, but Nicolo was excited, indeed, to find her royal page at his door a few days later.

"Her Highness requests the master violinist to play at the royal court, as soon as can be arranged," he announced solemnly.

"To play for a Princess! Why, Nico, it is the chance of a lifetime!" cried Germi who had returned from Genoa only the night before. "A good thing that I brought an extra supply of fiddle strings from Ricci."

Nicolo sighed. "Good, faithful Ricci. If only he could be here for the performance." He turned anxiously to Germi. "You gave him the Stradivarius for safe keeping?"

"In the vault it lies. And you should have heard him exclaim over your good fortune, Nico! As eager as a child he is to see the Guarnerius."

The concert evening arrived, and such a time as there was at the inn, getting ready for the event!

"The cream-colored knee breeches with the blue velvet coat will be the most elegant," decided Germi, pulling out boxes and scattering clothing in every direction. "And this white satin cravat–or perhaps the blue? No, the gold is best."

At last Nicolo was ready, handsome, indeed, in evening attire.

"I pay homage, my fine cockerel," laughed Germi, bowing low before his friend. "But come, or there'll be no homage at the palace if you keep the impatient ruler waiting!"

What an audience there was to greet Nicolo as he stepped onto the stage! Lords and ladies in finest costume sat in the royal boxes, with the Princess and her attendants well in the center.

Bowing low in her direction, Nicolo began to play. And with such power did he perform through the long evening, that again and again the audience broke into cheering.

"Master! Master! Paganini!" rang the calls.

The rare violin under his arm on the way home, Germi chuckled. "You have won the heart of the proud ruler with your music, Nico. And only once did she stop her listening, –just long enough to box the ears of her attendant for whispering!"

The very next morning, long before he had even thought of rising, the royal messenger was again at Nicolo's door.

"Up with you, man!" cried Germi, rushing into the sleeping quarters. "Your fortune is made! The Princess Elise receives Master Paganini in the royal suite this morning at eleven!"

Nothing in the world did Nicolo dislike as much as early rising. "Called from my rest at the bidding of a mere princess!" he muttered, pulling the covers over his head.

But Germi, well used to the whims of his friend, ripped the bedclothes from the shivering musician, calling, "Up! Up with you, man! Just one hour there is, to don your most fetching costume!"

Half asleep, Nicolo stumbled into his clothes. But once at the palace, he strode briskly behind the guard in his best morning coat and bowed low before the haughty Princess.

"Much pleasure you gave me with your music, Signor Paganini," she began, a smile playing about her lips. "And now that there is need of a director for the orchestra here at my court, I should like you to accept the position, young man."

An orchestra director! But it would mean giving up his own concerts. As he started to reply, Nicolo was silenced at once.

"It is not necessary to give thanks, Paganini," said the Princess. "I will expect you within the week. Good day, young man."

There was nothing to do but obey the royal command, and

soon Nicolo found himself in a small dark room at the court, treated as any other servant and with very little food to eat.

He sighed over the heavy duties: an orchestra to direct, music to write for special occasions, solos to play, and lessons to give to the royal Prince. Many new compositions were demanded by the Princess, who startled him one morning with a strange request.

"It is all very simple to play on four strings," said she. Pacing up and down the beautiful rooms, her jeweled bracelets gleamed on her white arms. "Compose something for me on one string alone," she commanded, "and when it is ready, come to me again."

Here was a challenge, indeed! At once he set to work in the night hours, the sound of his pen scratching through the little room. In less than a week he had finished an entire sonata and, with a twinkle in his eye, presented it to the ruler.

"So you have done what I thought was impossible!" exclaimed the Princess. " 'The Napoleon Sonata.' Well named, Paganini! Come, let us see what the music has to say."

When he had finished playing the fine composition, the Princess applauded heartily.

"An excellent work and worthy of your talents, Paganini," said she, and taking from her finger a heavy gold ring, she presented it to her concert master.

And now that the court had moved to the lovely old city of Florence, more music than ever was needed. Poor Nicolo! Not only was he weary, but he was hungry most of the time, as well. When he could stand it no longer, he spoke with the ruler, who flew into a rage at once.

"My good man, you do not seem to understand that you are a servant of the court, here to do my bidding!" she cried.

In quiet, firm tones, Nicolo answered swiftly.

"Your Highness," said he, "my duties as a musician go far beyond this court. I beg leave to play in other cities, where I will be well repaid for my services."

The Princess listened in surprise. Here was no weakling!

"Very well, Paganini," her voice was gentler now, "Your wish shall be granted. But see to it that you do not stay away too long!"

To be free again! Joyously Nicolo called for the faithful Germi, and what fine times they had, with rare evenings of music in cities nearby.

But always in his mind was the thought that he was still a servant of the court, and with a heavy heart, Nicolo went slowly back to Florence. Soon his duties were eating away the precious hours that went on into years. Would they never end?

One evening, at a very special court dinner, the Princess Elise glanced down at her concert master. He was leading the orchestra in afternoon uniform! Swiftly she turned to her attendant.

"Tell Paganini to change into evening attire at once!" she commanded.

Without stopping the music, Nicolo sent back his reply.

"My duties do not permit me to change at this hour," said he quietly.

Never was a princess angrier. Striking the table sharply with her fan, she exclaimed, "You may inform my haughty servant that after this evening's performance, we will have no further need of his services at court!"

Nicolo could hardly believe his ears. He was free at last, free of the prison where he had been forced to dwell for so long.

But careful—he must not show his pleasure. Frowning, he led the next number with such speed that the men could scarcely follow him. What had come over their leader?

Finished at last! Quickly packing his belongings, he rushed out into the dark courtyard.

"Mario!" he called. "I must get away at once. Hasten, my good man!"

As they drove off into the night, the moon shone on Nicolo's pale, thin face, alive now with joy. His long legs beat a merry dance on the floorboards as he sang at the top of his voice.

"I am free! free! free!" he warbled. "I am coming, oh, world. Paganini is free!"

Suddenly the singing stopped as Nicolo turned to the driver.

"You do not share my joy, Mario. All is not well with you?"

The driver looked straight ahead, trying to hide his sorrow.

"It is my Maria, Signor. Long years she waited for the little one, only to have it taken from her. Night and day she mourns the small creature, and nothing can bring her peace."

Nicolo laid his hand on the driver's shoulder. "I did not know. Forgive my foolish chatter."

A few miles beyond, a faint light glimmered by the roadside, and Mario pulled on the reins. "My humble dwelling, sir. You would not mind if I look in on my Maria? Come, too, if you like."

As the two crept into the small cottage, the low sound of weeping came from the darkness.

"It is always so," whispered Mario. "If only I could comfort her!"

Nicolo waited quietly in the tiny kitchen, the low murmur of voices in the room beyond drifting into the night. Then, hardly knowing why he did so, he took out his violin and began to play a lullaby. Gentle as a breath, the melody stole to the next room, –warm and tender and soothing. The liquid tones became one with the night as Nicolo played on, the peaceful compositions melting one into another.

Without a sound, he put his fiddle away and was startled to find someone standing near him.

"You have cured her, sir," murmured Mario, happy tears in his dark eyes. "She will get well now. Sleep has already come."

On into the starry night rode the two men, silent now and with a deep peace in them.

But already in Nicolo's mind a new composition was forming, and as the darkness faded into the glory of morning, he could hardly wait to get to the inn to set down the dancing notes. Much new music would be needed for concerts, now that he was free.

And concerts there were, through all of Italy, and his fame grew with the months. In Milan, alone, thirty-six musical evenings there were in one year, and the name of Paganini was on every lip.

And now, wherever he went to play, everyone began to study the violin. But no matter how they tried, no one could make tones like the master.

"He has a magic power! Some say that sparks fly from his fingers when they touch the strings. We must discover his secrets!" the whispers went round.

They set to work in earnest, watching his every movement. Whenever Nicolo went out for a little airing, someone was close at his heels. In his room, prying eyes were always at the keyhole.

One morning, rising later than usual, he called at once for the waiter. "Never have I been so hungry! Bring all the food you have, my good man."

Wrapping himself in a warm dressing gown, Nicolo began to hum as he helped himself to the tempting hot breakfast. The world was a good place, after all! Pushing away the table, he reached for his violin and began to play, when a sharp rustling disturbed him.

"Bother!" he cried. "Swallows again! A fire, Giorgio," he called to the servant. "The smoke will send the birds out into the sun, and we will have done with their scratching noises."

No sooner was the kindling ablaze than a loud scraping began inside the chimney. With a heavy thud, a man fell into the flames, sending them flying in all directions.

"Upon my soul!" cried Nicolo, as the frightened creature scrambled to his feet. "Spying again! Will I never be rid of it?"

The poor man stood before him, trembling in terror as he wiped the soot from his eyes and mouth.

Ah well, he had been punished enough, thought Nicolo, and going to the door, he opened it wide. Clattering headlong down the stairs, the tattered man raced through the streets as if Satan were after him, while Nicolo leaned from the window, laughing until he ached as he watched the amazed townfolk scurry from the pathway of the blackened runaway.

The warm summer months crept over the beautiful Italian countryside, and joyously Nicolo took himself off to the quiet monastery of Certosa. No one would find him here.

In old clothes he tramped over the drowsy hills and meadows, and back through the lovely gardens where the brown-robed monks were busy with their chores. Under an old cypress he lay in the cooling shade and, smiling with contentment, was soon in the land of dreams.

But in a few days he was ready to work again. Long hours he spent in finding new ways of playing the violin. Two and even three notes he sounded together, and difficult high parts in double tones, undreamed of before.

The quiet, gentle life filled him with peace, bringing the beautiful "Prayer from Moses" from his pen.

But always at sunset, while the brothers walked in the gardens, Nicolo played his loveliest music for them. The heavenly melodies stole through the rose-colored light, bringing them close to his cell window. There they stood, scarcely moving as they drank in the glory and beauty of sound.

The cool, fresh days of autumn came all too soon, and bidding good-bye to his peaceful hideaway, Nicolo was off in the battered old coach. As the miles rolled away, bright life began to stir within him. How good it was to be out in the world again!

Arriving in lovely Florence, he smiled happily at finding a letter from his good friend Rossini, the composer.

"Come and join us for the carnival. Meyerbeer and I await you."

Carnival in Rome! With a cry of delight, Nicolo was off again, rumbling northward along the rutted roads.

My, what a greeting there was in the fine old city!

"As fit as a fiddle you are, Nicolo!" cried Rossini, leading his friend to the beautiful rooms that he and the composer, Meyerbeer, had arranged with such care.

"You have done all this for me?" exclaimed Nicolo, looking happily at the fine new clavier and bouquets of loveliest flowers.

"When a royal visitor honors us with his presence, he must

have a royal home. But now to the carnival! Your costume, Nicolo!"

Pushing through the crowds, three strangely dressed women in feathered bonnets whirled down the streets, their eyes carefully hidden. Finding a small opening, the tallest raised a violin to her shoulder and began a plaintive song, the second joining her on the guitar. The third, taking her hat from her matted hair, passed it to the listeners, singing in quavering tones:

> "Three poor old beggarwomen are we,
> Fill our small basket, if you please."

How well the beggars played—especially the violinist!

Suddenly a voice in the crowd shouted, "Paganini!"

Instantly there was an uproar, and in a flash the three women disappeared into the crowd, to search for a new place for their begging.

After frolicking to their heart's content, and weary with dancing and laughter, the three famous musicians hid themselves away in Rossini's rooms for a feast of music.

Nicolo sighed as he pulled off his costume.

"Ah, my good friends, well you know that the heart of Paganini can be shown to you in only one way. You asked for an account of me. Now you shall have it."

Reaching for a violin, he tested it quickly. "Put out the lights, please," he commanded.

With the street lamps making patterns dance and flicker on the ceiling, Nicolo began to play. The full, rich tones cried out in the night, telling of the loneliness in the heart of a great musician. The friends, carried away by the sheer beauty, listened to the melodies which rose and fell in waves of loveliest sound.

When the music came to an end, a tumult of cheering rose from the street below.

"An audience!" exclaimed Nicolo. "Is it never possible to escape?"

Rossini answered gently from the darkness. "As long as Paganini touches the strings of a violin, magic will stir the hearts of men."

Nicolo strode to the window and stared down at the large crowd.

"Help me, Gioacchino!" he cried. "You must get me back to my fine quarters. Quickly, by the back stairway!"

"If only that were possible," sighed his friend. "But look you, Nicolo, —there is the costume! They will never discover you."

The crowds were still waiting for a glimpse of the great musician an hour later, when the dawn was beginning to light the streets of Rome. Quietly they made way for a thin, bent old woman hobbling along on her cane, her face well hidden in a bonnet tied under her chin.

A few days later, after he had played in the Cathedral, Nicolo was proud, indeed, to be made a Knight of the Golden Spur. And what a celebration there was that evening in the beautiful quarters!

"Grand Cavalier, we beg you to accept the place of honor,"

said the hosts solemnly, leading Nicolo to the head of the groaning table, piled high with every delicacy.

"Come, come, my fine comrades!" laughed the guest. "You will have me so spoiled that never again will I enjoy my simple life!"

But all through the banquet, Rossini was strangely quiet, and when a long sigh escaped his lips, Nicolo turned to him quickly.

"What is wrong, Gioacchino? You have scarcely touched this food."

Rossini stared down at his plate. "I did not want you to know," he began slowly. "It is my opera. In just two weeks it must be ready, and the orchestra parts are hardly begun. It is no use. I could never finish it in time."

In an instant Nicolo was on his feet.

"Clear away the banquet!" he ordered. "And now for the music. Bring it at once, Gioacchino!"

Through the days and nights the friends worked with all their strength, and a short time before the opera was to be given, Nicolo gave his next command.

"Bring the orchestra and the singers together. I will rehearse them while you finish the opening music, Gioacchino," he cried, hurrying away to the Opera House.

On the very night of the performance, the last bit of the music was learned, and rushing to their rooms, the two friends dressed in frantic haste and were soon back at the hall.

"How could I ever thank you, Nicolo?" began Gioacchino as the people poured into the Opera House.

"Thank me? Why, when I am an old man with white whiskers, you will do as much for me, my dear fellow! But see—it is time that you were back stage. Quickly, Gioacchino!"

The signal had come, and Nicolo stood in the pit to lead the orchestra. But even in the half darkness, the audience caught sight of him, and a startled whisper went round.

"Paganini!"

What a success the opera turned out to be! Again and again there were calls for the composer, and going to the stage amid a burst of applause, Rossini turned directly to Nicolo, bowing his head in solemn thanks.

Well pleased with his adventures in Rome, Nicolo began the journey up to Milan. After a few concerts, he would go back to Genoa to see what was wrong with his dearest possession.

The Guarnerius violin had not sounded well lately, with a hoarseness creeping into the tone that worried him. But Ricci would find the trouble. Faithful Ricci! Sighing, Nicolo settled the case more comfortably on his knees. Never was it out of his sight.

Arriving in Milan, he went at once to a small inn and, after a cup of tea, crept into bed and was soon asleep. But in the middle of the night he awakened with a chill, and by morning, he was ill, indeed.

"A horrible disease you must have, Signori" cried the inn-keeper, wringing his hands in alarm. "You will have to leave my house at once!"

Nicolo, his face flushed with a high fever, stared up at the man, hardly believing what he had heard.

"But I am too ill to be moved, sir," he moaned. "Later–later my good fellow."

But his words were of no avail.

"Up with you, man!" shouted the keeper. "Out of my house this minute!"

Trembling, Nicolo pulled on his clothing and felt his way to the steps. But his legs refused to carry him farther, and he sat down suddenly, his black hat falling over his eyes.

A few minutes later, a voice startled him from his dreaming.

"Paganini!" The cellist from the orchestra bent down to look into his face. "You are ill, man!" he cried. "What are you doing out here in the cold?"

With a sigh, Nicolo muttered, "Landlord–disease."

"He put you out of the house?"

Ciandelli did not wait for a reply. An eye peeking through a crack told him all.

"Scoundrel!" he shouted and, flinging open the door, dragged the cowering innkeeper to the roadway. Seizing Nicolo's cane, he beat him all the way down the street, the man howling with pain as he ran for his life.

As ill as he was, Nicolo laughed until the tears ran down his cheeks.

"Never again will he turn a sick man away, I'll wager!" panted the cellist, his eyes still flashing with bitter anger.

Quickly he took his patient to a quiet resting place, watching over him with the greatest care until he was well again.

"You have saved my life, my good friend," smiled Nicolo. "What could I ever do to repay you?"

"Repay me!" the startled words rang out. "Your music has done that, a thousand times over," replied Ciandelli.

But Nicolo could not be content. At once he began to give lessons to the cellist, who had had such a hard time keeping his little family together. In not too long a time, he was delighted to be giving concerts of his own. And not only did he make a name for himself in the musical world, but a good living besides, thanks to Paganini.

But now Nicolo was becoming more and more worried as he listened to the tone of the Guarnerius. It was changing rapidly, indeed, and so muffled that there was no longer joy in playing on the instrument.

In despair he paced the floor through the days and most of the nights. No food would he take, and his friends were sorely upset.

"You cannot go on like this!" they cried. "Why not go down to Ricci at once and see what can be done?"

Nicolo looked at the faithful group with hollow eyes.

"But my concert of next week?" he questioned.

"It can wait. To Genoa–and Ricci!" the cry went round.

The next moment the room was turned upside down as the friends began the packing. Nicolo was hurried into his coat, and down the stairs after him trouped the four.

A strong wind had piled the clouds in heavy black masses overhead, and Nicolo listened uneasily as the gale shouted its warning. At any moment now, the storm would break and churn the roads into heavy thick mud.

Would he ever reach Genoa and his good friend, Ricci?

CHAPTER FIVE

Nicolo took his place in the carriage and shivered as the driving rain struck hard at the windows. Wrapping his fur coat more closely around him, he settled himself against the cushions, his eyes brooding under his tall black hat.

His troubles grew with the miles, and he sighed often as the coach lumbered along the slippery roadway. If anything serious was wrong with the Guarnerius, his concerts might be at an end, for not even the Stradivarius suited his kind of playing. At the very thought, he groaned aloud, and the passengers looked at the stranger with pity. In all the long hours of traveling, he had spoken no word and eaten not a mouthful of food.

A little old woman opened her basket and timidly touched his arm. "You will have a sausage, sir, with a bit of bread and wine?"

Nicolo stared at her and slowly shook his head.

"You are kind, but I do not feel hunger," said he.

The carriage jolted and creaked along, sliding through slippery mud and falling into deep pools of water. But at last the storm was at an end. How good it was to see the sun smiling from the clean blue heavens when they arrived in Genoa!

Stumbling from the coach, Nicolo's long legs took him with all haste to Ricci's little shop in the square.

"The master—he is not here?" he cried in alarm, looking anxiously about him. But soon his fears were at an end.

"Nico!" In hobbled the little workman, bent with years, a blanket thrown over his thin shoulders. One look at his visitor told him that all was not well.

"The violin?" he asked, his fingers already on the lock.

"Oh, master—the tone that I loved so well is gone!"

This was serious, indeed! With expert hands, Ricci hastily examined the instrument and laid it down gently.

"I believe I have found the trouble, Nico. Inside, a section has come unglued. The fiddle must be taken apart at once."

A sharp cry of alarm came from Nicolo's lips.

"Ruined forever!" he exclaimed. "It would never be the same again!"

The little man looked up quickly. "But there is no other way to reach the trouble." Quietly he put his hand on Nicolo's arm. "You must promise not to come while we are opening the instrument."

But the next morning, pale and shaken, Nicolo was again in the shop.

"I could not stay away, Ricci," he explained slowly. "The violin is my life. If anything goes wrong, I can never play again."

The master spoke kindly. "Courage, my friend," said he. "The worst will soon be over." Briskly he turned to the boys. "Close the doors at once, and see that the windows are well barred. Then we can begin."

With bated breath, Nicolo sat in a chair as Ricci began to pry the cover from the rare instrument. With a loud crack the varnish broke, and Nicolo sprang to his feet, his hands to his ears.

"Ah, just as I thought, –here is the trouble," explained Ricci happily, putting down his tools. "See–a loosened lining! You can safely leave the rest to me, my friend. Better get some fresh air now. And a little sleep will do you no harm."

While the weeks of mending were going on, Nicolo was busy, indeed. Quietly he moved his family to a fine new house, high on the hill. "And see that there are plenty of beds and warm blankets," he directed.

"Why, Nico!" exclaimed his mother. "They are just the things you dreamed of having when you were a little boy." She sighed happily, smoothing her new black dress over her tired knees. "So many blessings you have brought us with your music, my son."

The three weeks of waiting were like years to poor Nicolo. But the moment he caught sight of Ricci's face, his fears were over.

"As good as new, my boy!" cried the workman with a smile, putting the instrument into the eager hands.

A few bold strokes of the bow told him that all was well, and throwing his arms about the little man, Nicolo pulled him around the shop in a merry dance as tears of joy rolled down his pale cheeks.

"Bravo, Ricci, bravo!" he shouted. "You have given me back my very life!"

What a flood of golden tone poured from the heart of the fine old instrument as the months rolled by! And now, his mind and heart at ease, Nicolo decided to accept the invitation of Prince Metternich, who had heard him play in

Rome. Yes, it would be quite an adventure to play for the people of Vienna.

But a sudden thought made him pause. How would he get along in a country whose language was so different from his own? Ah well, surely everyone would understand the language of music.

Humming a merry tune, he took out the shabby case housing the violin. In one end he put a few jewels and his watch—in the other, some linen. A small battered bag held his extra clothing and a black box, his evening hat.

The little packing was quickly finished, and he was on his way to Austria, for the first time leaving his native land. But arriving at the border, he was uneasy as the men of the customs eyed him sharply.

"A strange visitor we have here," said the officer to his helper. "So thin he is and how white his skin—almost like wax."

"Yes, and notice his eyes—so piercing under those shaggy dark brows. Come, Franz, we must find out about this newcomer to Austria."

Shoulders erect, they marched to the stranger, speaking rapidly in German. "Your traveling papers, sir!" they demanded crisply.

Poor Nicolo! In dismay he looked up at the men.

"I—I am Paganini," he answered meekly.

"Paganini, the great violinist!" exclaimed the officers, talking rapidly now in his own tongue. "Come, good sir—you must have a special room where you can rest before you go on with your journey."

Food and drink were brought at once to the noted visitor, and an hour later Nicolo started on his way in a fine new coach, richly padded in deep red velvet.

"Not a bad beginning in a strange country!" laughed Nicolo to the old driver as they rolled merrily along.

An even greater surprise was awaiting him when he arrived in the old city of Vienna. There, gathered around the inn, was a large crowd, and as the coach door was opened, a rousing cheer went up.

"Welcome to our city, Signor Paganini," greeted a city official in red robes of state. "All Austria has awaited your coming with eagerness, and we hope that you will be at home among us."

The band struck up a merry waltz, and dancing throngs whirled around Nicolo as he was led into the inn.

Never had he dreamed of such a welcome by the Austrian people. And never could he have dreamed of what was to happen after his first concert. From that evening on, wherever he walked, his portrait stared at him from every shop window. There were hats, dresses, shoes, perfumes, and gloves "a-la-Paganini." Dainty dishes were named for him, and his picture was on all walking sticks and snuff boxes.

Again and again he played for cheering audiences, and his name grew more famous with the days. The Waltz King, Strauss, wrote special Paganini waltzes; Schumann and Brahms, the great composers, wrote music from themes of Nicolo's own works, while Mendelssohn sang his praises, night and day.

One morning, as he was dressing, Nicolo heard a loud noise in the hallway outside and, quickly opening the door, found a servant dragging a poor man toward the stairs.

"One word with the master, I pray you!" he begged. "One little word will mean life itself to me!"

Quietly Nicolo walked to the trembling creature. "What is it that you wish to say to me?" he asked gently.

With a cry of joy, the shabby visitor fell to his knees, eager words pouring from his lips:

"Oh master, I am only the poor driver, Jehu, known to everyone in Vienna. If only you will allow me to print something on my cab, my little ones will be saved from hunger."

"And what would you like to print on your cab?"

"Just two words, master: 'Cab Paganini.' And with your permission in this paper, 'Cab Paganini' will take you wherever you wish to go, day or night, city or country, free of charge!"

Jehu lost no time in getting his cab in order. And so many were there to ride in his 'Cab Paganini' that soon Jehu became very rich, indeed. At once he bought himself an inn, drawing to his Hotel Paganini more visitors than it would hold.

Nicolo loved to wander along the back streets of the city and listen to the little bands and singers that were everywhere. How the people of Vienna loved music!

Late one afternoon as he was strolling happily with a friend, he spied a ragged boy across the roadway, sawing away on a tiny violin.

"One of your countrymen, Paganini, and in need," declared his companion.

In a moment Nicolo was beside the young musician. Emptying his pockets of coins into the worn cap on the ground, he took the poor fiddle from the small hands and swept the bow over the strings.

"Paganini! It is the master who plays!" whispered the startled listeners, while the little Italian boy could only stare in wonder.

Taking his hat from his head, Nicolo passed it through the crowd for the bright shower of tinkling coins. Without a word he poured them into the small cap and, patting the boy's tousled locks, went on his way down the street.

The next morning he was up earlier than usual and, with his secretary, Harris, beside him in the carriage, started out for a nearby city, where a special concert was to be given.

The roads were poor, indeed, and at midday, stopping for fresh horses, he was happy to move about with the other passengers, glad of a little airing.

But before he knew it, Nicolo was far down the roadway, and coming upon a pretty little village, he exclaimed in delight. Nothing did he like more than exploring, and through the streets he wandered, smiling and nodding and putting coins into the hands of bright-eyed children.

Happy and content, he started back toward the carriage, when who should come running to meet him but Harris, his long arms waving in the air.

"It is gone, sir!" he panted. "Only a little nap I took, and when I awoke, the carriage had left without us!"

Nicolo was angry and, pacing up and down the roadway, shook his stick after the coach. As suddenly he grew calm.

"Hire horses at once, Harris!" he commanded. "We must go on quickly, to be in time for the concert."

The secretary looked at him anxiously. "I have already tried, sir, but there are none to be had."

"Then we must walk," decided Nicolo, picking up the violin case.

"But thirty miles, sir!" groaned Harris. "We could never do it—never!"

Late that night they arrived in the next city, to find the concert hall tightly locked and everyone in bed for the night. In despair the two men found a room and, weary, fell into sound sleep.

The next morning early, Nicolo hurried to the manager, to find him smiling and calm.

"Ah, Paganini, always there can be the accident," said he. "So I just tell the people, 'He is not here. Come tomorrow, instead!' "

With a cry of relief, Nicolo kissed the man heartily on both cheeks. And what a concert he gave the people that night–one that they were never to forget, their whole lives long.

Delighted with concerts in the Austrian capitol, Nicolo decided to play through all of Germany, and soon he was on his way. Everywhere he was treated as a king, and audiences forgot to applaud, so lost were they in his glorious music.

In Hamburg, after the last great work was ended, the noted poet, Heine, ran to his side, showering him with praise.

"Ah, Paganini, you should be proud, indeed, to give such rich blessings to others," he exclaimed, clasping his hand.

"Proud?" Nicolo raised shaggy brows. "Now that is something I do not understand. But tell me, Herr Heine, how did you like my bowing to the audience?"

Always seeking new adventures, Nicolo took himself to the great city of London. And how surprised he was to find that he was already well known, crowds in the street following him wherever he went.

Prices for the first concert were doubled, and many were given, so that all the people might see and hear the great master of the strings. Each time that he played, tall police guards took him safely through the cheering throngs.

Children were everywhere, and Nicolo smiled as they ran up to him, touching him quickly and racing back to their parents.

"Is it a game that the little ones play with me?" he asked a red-coated guard at his side.

The man laughed shortly. "Not quite, Master Paganini. It is to see if you are real. You see, it is said that you have powers given only to creatures of another world!"

Each day, more and more invitations had come from the French people, begging him to play for them. But the very thought sent little shivers up and down the master's spine. The greatest music center in all the world was there, where the leading artists of the day were gathered together.

Yes, it was in the city of Paris that his real test as a musician would come.

With strange feelings, Nicolo made himself ready one afternoon. On the following day, he would cross the water and try his luck in the great French capital.

CHAPTER SIX

Never was there a stormier day along the English Channel. Paganini looked up at the dark clouds racing over his head and felt the gray mist brush against his white cheeks. As the waters struck hard against the little boat, he groaned aloud. Would they ever reach the shores of France?

Gently pushing away the hot broth, held to his lips by a seaman at his side, he peered for a moment at the whitecapped waves, lashed into a fury by the March wind.

"Soon, now, we will be safely ashore, sir," comforted the steward, wrapping the black fur coat more closely around his famous passenger.

"A lifetime!" groaned Nicolo. "And never again will I set foot in a boat—never!"

But it was not long before he had forgotten all his troubles in the bustling French capital. With the greatest joy he rode through the gay city, alive with merry chatter and silvery laughter.

So this was Paris!

Gathered under its rooftops were more famous authors, painters, musicians, than in any other center of the world.

"Ah, Signor Paganini—you are here at last!" the concert manager greeted him warmly. "Such a nice little place I have found for you. But come, you shall see for yourself."

Nicolo was delighted with the sunny rooms looking out over the River Seine, with a beautiful new clavier by the window, ready for use. Before an hour had passed, he was settled, and out along the river he strolled, back to the small office near the Opera House.

"Paganini!" the manager looked up in surprise. "I did not expect you for a week!" At once he was serious. "We must not hurry the first concert, to give plenty of time for the practicing."

"Practicing!" exclaimed Nicolo, smiling. "That I have not done in more than seventeen years, sir!"

The manager could not believe his ears. A word of warning might be helpful to this newcomer to Paris.

"Signor Paganini," he began thoughtfully, "it is no simple matter to play in this city. The greatest artists of all the world will be in your audience. They will be severe critics, my good man."

The smile had not left the master's face. "All are welcome," said he, "quietly. "Shall we have the first concert next week?"

The manager sprang to his feet, his hands clasping nervously. "Surely you could not be ready in so short a time, Signor!"

Paganini looked at him calmly. "I could be ready tomorrow, or even tonight, if there was need," he answered quietly.

The March wind thundered through the city on the special evening, shaking the rain from heavy black clouds. But every seat in the beautiful Opera House was taken as Nicolo, in his best black coat, arrived with his battered violin case under his arm.

What a sight greeted him as he moved into the spacious entrance hall! Breathless, he stood in a corner, the gleaming crystal chandeliers lighting the colorful scene around him.

"Like a fairy tale!" he whispered, as elegantly-dressed men and women moved up the great white marble staircases carpeted in rich red velvet. Smiling happily, he went quickly behind the stage.

Quietly he listened as the orchestra music came to a close. It was time, now, for him to appear! His greatest test as a musician was at hand. Taking a deep breath, he glided onto the stage and bowed as a wave of applause greeted him.

"So this is Paganini! But how delicate he looks. A wonder that he has strength to play!" the whispers sounded here and there.

When all was still, Nicolo nodded to the conductor, and the music of his own composing began. Deep and rich, the melting tones swept over the audience, weaving a magic spell.

There was a long sigh as the first movement came to an end. In hushed silence the people sat without moving, waiting breathlessly for the concerto to continue.

With a sweep of the bow, Nicolo struck the strings fast and hard, and a shower of notes, like stars, sprang from the instrument. Cries of astonishment echoed through the house as the audience watched, spellbound.

Now he was plucking the strings rapidly between long strokes of the bow. Like a solo with guitar accompaniment it sounded. Never before had there been such playing in the city of Paris.

The audience was in an uproar, and rushing backstage, musicians and critics crowded around the great master, trying to discover his secrets.

"For the first time, the violin sings in all its glory!" cried the noted pianist and composer, Franz Liszt. "Never have I heard such sadness, such joy from four slender strings!"

"Ah yes, yes!" agreed the master, Cherubini. "I shall not be able to sleep, for thinking of these songs of the strings."

"Sh! Sh! He comes!" the whispers gave the warning as Paganini appeared for the second part of the program.

Plucking the strings lightly, to make sure they were in tune, the master stood ready, and the orchestra music began. Raising his violin to his shoulder, he played a few notes when snap! a string broke with a loud noise.

A gasp of dismay came from the audience. What would happen now?

Without waiting a moment, Nicolo nodded to the

conductor and went on at once, playing as easily on three strings as on four! And when, near the end of the program, the second and third strings broke, the people could not believe their eyes. There before them stood the great artist, performing on one string alone an entire composition, his "Prayer from Moses!"

Excited cries, and waves of cheering, and stamping stopped the playing again and again. A miracle had been performed that night in the Opera House of Paris.

After his first concert, the name of Paganini was on every lip. Everything in the city was named for him, even to hairdressing and roast beef "a-la-Paganini." At all hours of the day, a steady stream of visitors was at his door. Invitations and gifts there were without end, and Nicolo shook his head in amazement.

"I shall have to set up a museum for my treasures," he declared, "or be poor in carrying them around with me!"

How the printers swarmed around him, begging him for his compositions and asking how they were composed.

"Why not give us your Sonatas and Concertos, your Variations and Quartets and Caprices, so that everyone may have them to play?" they asked, hovering over the master.

At their words, Nicolo leaped from his chair, his dark eyes flashing. "And you would have everyone know my secrets of playing the violin?" he cried, storming about the room. "I say to you: No, gentlemen!" Then as suddenly, a smile lighted his face. "You asked me how I compose. Well now, that is very simple. A story comes into my mind, and I tell it in melody. That is all."

Happy times there were for Nicolo, but lonely times, as well. Often his thoughts wandered to Italy and the beautiful singer, Bianchi, and their young son, Achille. The boy would have a few years behind him now. How he longed to see him again!

Nicolo sighed over his simple breakfast. Ah yes, it would be good to have the child with him. But it would mean giving up his concerts. Concerts! Always they had kept him from home.

And now it was time to go back to England, and soon the master was on his way. How he liked the English people! With the greatest joy he played for them, and then on to Scotland and Ireland he journeyed to the great crowds gathered to hear him.

Any sum that he asked was given without a murmur, and Nicolo grew very rich, indeed, as the months rolled by.

But many days there were when he was far from well, and the simplest food gave him pain. A bowl of soup or a cup of chocolate was his only breakfast; a cup of chamomile tea was his supper. But when traveling, not a bite of food did he take until his journey was at an end.

Letters from France or Italy gave him the greatest joy, and over and over he read them until he knew them by heart.

"Come back! Come back to us!" called the French people, after their favorite violinist had been away from them for a whole year.

Nicolo chuckled. "So there are real friends, after all!" he declared, his face in a warm glow. "Why have I stayed away so long?"

How warmly he was welcomed in the city of Paris! Parties there were without number, with the guests swarming about their dear Paganini, whose simple manners charmed them all.

"Come, Nicolo, tell us a story!" the call would go around.

With a smile, the master would begin. Waving his long arms, he spoke in such a mixture of English, Italian, German, and French, that howls of laughter drowned out his words.

"Always those words—they are too difficult for me. But in music, I can say what is in my mind and heart."

The moment he reached for his violin, there was instant silence. Then someone would whisper: "Perpetual Motion!" or "Witches Dance!"

Never was there a concert or party where he was not asked to play his compositions that raced with such breathless speed as to leave everyone gasping when they came to a close. How could anyone play music so difficult?

To Nicolo, it was child's play, and each time sounded as fresh as though he had never performed them before. Ah yes, it was all very well to play for his friends in any kind of room. But outside, all must be exactly to his liking.

Late one morning after his simple meal, he was startled to find a messenger from the court at his door.

"There will be a notable gathering at the Tuileries Gardens, Master Paganini. The Council begs your services for the evening's entertainment," he announced, with a stiff little bow.

The morning of the special event arrived, and off hurried Nicolo to the room where he was to play. Looking in dismay at the heavy curtains and rugs, he gave a sharp command to the officer at his side.

"These must all be removed at once!" he declared. "They would eat up the tones of the violin, and no one would hear my playing."

But the pompous official did not agree and strutted about the gardens until time for the people to gather.

With a flourish of trumpets, the royal guests arrived with their attendants and took their places in the splendid hall.

What an evening they would have, with the famous Paganini to play for them!

It was time, now, for the concert to begin. But as the minutes passed by and no artist appearing, murmurs began to arise. Anxiously the official searched for the violinist, but he was nowhere to be found.

"Quickly—to the master's dwelling!" he ordered the messenger. "Something dreadful must have happened!"

On winged feet the page sped down the street and, out of breath, knocked loudly on Paganini's door.

"Sh! Quiet, please!" cautioned the servant, finger on lips. "You seek the great violinist? No, he has not gone out. He went to bed very early and does not wish to be disturbed. Goodnight, sir."

Concerts and honors came to Nicolo with the days. But nothing could compare with the joyous news that arrived one morning. Through the rooms he ran, waving a letter over his head.

"Josef! Josef!" he called to the servant. "He comes! My little Achille is on his way to Paris! Quickly–make ready this room next to mine. He may be here any minute now!"

The master could hardly wait and spent the hours in filling the room with toys, brought from the finest shops in the city.

At last, late one afternoon, carriage wheels sounded on the driveway, and with a bound, Nicolo was at the door. Gazing in delight at the small passenger in fitted red coat, he put out his hand in welcome.

"Achille!" Nicolo's eyes were bright with tears as he held the short fingers in his great palm. "Such a little fellow you

were when last I saw you—scarcely more than a pocketful! And now we will make up for these years that concerts have kept me away from you, eh, little one?"

With a joyous laugh he swept the boy into his long arms and carried him into the brightly-lighted rooms. Never, in all of his years, was he as happy as at this very moment.

For days he would not let the boy out of his sight, taking him everywhere to call on his friends. And when anyone stopped him on the street to speak of his playing, he would exclaim:

"Ah yes, yes, you are very kind. But have you seen my greatest treasure? Come, Achillino, and shake hands with the gentleman. Just look into his eyes, sir. Is he not a wise boy for his years? Another concert? Soon—soon. And my son will be in the front seat, listening to his father. A fine evening we will have, yes, Achillino?"

Of the many composers in Paris, Nicolo admired the master, Berlioz, and was sad to learn that he was far from well, and in great need. Hearing that he would be present when one of his new compositions was to be played, Nicolo hurried to the hall through the wintry night.

Listening closely to the fine work, he applauded heartily. Then, quietly taking himself to the stage where the master stood before the audience, Nicolo knelt at his feet and kissed his hand.

"My homage, Master Berlioz," said he, "and my humble thanks for the great joy that your music has given me."

A few days later, he was in the poor rooms of the composer, to find the master with a wracking cough, a worn shawl about his shoulders. Nicolo shivered in the poor quarters. Here was poverty, indeed.

"I am in need of a solo for my Stradivarius viola, Master,"

he explained. "If you could find time to write one for me, I would be greatly honored."

Berlioz smiled and looked sharply at his visitor.

"An excellent composer like you, asking another to write a composition? That is a compliment, indeed!" He sighed and pulled the shawl closer about his thin shoulders. "Very well. I will do what I can to please you," said he. "And when the work begins to take form, I will call you."

But never was the solo written, for it turned into a beautiful symphony, instead, which Berlioz called "Harold in Italy." With all haste, Nicolo sent the master a large sum of money, telling him how much he enjoyed the fine work that had come from his pen.

And now, after six full years away, a longing grew in the heart of Paganini for a resting place of his own in his beloved Italy. One day, when he could bear it no longer, he called to the servant, a new light in his eyes.

"Pack at once! I am going home!" he cried. "Home, do you hear? Paganini is going home!"

And what a coach he ordered for the journey, –the inside richly tufted in sky-blue satin.

Achille, who was dressed warmly for the long journey,

stood on the steps, his eyes round with delight.

"We go home in style, eh, my little prince!" Nicolo laughed joyously. "Climb in, small one, and we can be off."

Over the poor roads they rumbled, Nicolo chatting away and telling stories day in and day out until at last they arrived at the border of Italy. His heart overflowing with joy, he flung open the window of the carriage.

"Achillino! Lean your head out, child, and fill your lungs with the sun-kissed air of Italy!" he cried to the drowsy boy. "Tell me, little one, does it not smell sweeter than any you have known?"

But the cold air, racing into the carriage, startled Achille. Pulling the warm robe around his neck, he snuggled back into the cushions. But his father did not notice, and when they touched the edge of Genoa, out he leaped, lifting the boy to the ground.

"Feel the dust on your shoes, child!" he exclaimed, tramping about excitedly. "It is the sacred soil of Genoa, the birthplace of your own father! We are at home, Achillino, home at last!"

The driver brushed the tears from his eyes with his coat sleeve as he listened to the hungry words. On he urged the patient horses through the winding streets to the Passage of the Black Cat.

"Softly! Step softly here!" said the master, climbing the long stone stairway. "In this very room I was born, little one. And see, –here is where I learned to play the violin, practicing such long, long hours."

He stopped suddenly, looking down into the soft brown eyes. "Never was there enough bread to stay the hunger. Ah, my son," he cried, gathering the boy close, "never will you know what it means to be poor!"

Now a very rich man, Nicolo looked carefully about for a fitting place to live. One day, just outside Parma, he came upon a fine old stone villa, lying peacefully among the green hills beside a lake.

"We have found it, Achillino!" he cried happily. "Here we will stay all our lives long!"

At once, glass cases were built to house the rare instruments that had been given him through the years, and long hours the master hovered over them each day, keeping them in perfect tune.

When visitors came from far and near to bring him honor, Paganini sometimes played a little on the fine Amati or the

Stradivarius violin. But when he had put them down, his dark eyes would glow as he reached for his favorite Guarnerius.

"Now the king of them all will speak to you, and from heaven itself," he would say in hushed voice.

Closing his eyes, he would gently touch the strings, smiling as the rich golden tones flowed into the room. All of his cares were at once forgotten as he dwelt in a world all his own.

One morning, as he was about to leave his room, he heard a great noise outside, with servants running past his door.

"It is the little one, sir! He has fallen and hurt the leg!" cried the faithful Giulia, wringing her hands at the terror in her master's face.

"A doctor!" shouted Paganini, rushing headlong through the rooms. "Bring two doctors—all the doctors in Parma!"

Through the long hours that followed, he never left the bedside of his son, talking in low, soothing tones to quiet the restless figure. But with all his striving, the aching was too strong, and Achille tossed and turned as the pain struck at him.

"The leg must be still, Master Paganini," said the doctor, "or the broken bones cannot knit together."

What was there to do? Nicolo held his head in his hands. Suddenly he stood up, alert.

"Come, Giulia," said he, seating himself in an easy chair by the window. "Place the boy here, on my knees, and we shall see what happens."

Almost at once the whimpering ceased, and with his head on his father's shoulder, the tired young eyes closed in sleep, the first in many hours.

Through the long days and nights, Nicolo sat with the child, scarcely breathing as he slept and soothing his fretful waking hours. Stories and songs flowed from his lips without end, to keep the leg still.

For eight days and nights the master held his precious burden, and at last the doctor smiled.

"All is well. The bones have knit," he announced. "And a good rest is ordered for you at once, Master Paganini, or we shall have another patient on our hands."

Now that the leg was getting better, what fine times there were in the long sunny days. Achille's merry laughter echoed through the house as he watched his father scramble about on all fours, performing tricks or acting out plays.

Giulia, looking into the room, shook her head in despair. Only a few moments before, all had been in order. Now, everything was turned upside down, with toys scattered everywhere.

"Toys!" she whispered to her helper, Toni. "And still others, in every room of the house. If the master brings in more, we shall all have to move out!"

Now there were very few concerts for Paganini, and whenever he was asked to perform, he would say with a smile, "Fifty years of playing is not enough? Surely I have earned a little rest from the fiddle."

Most of all, he loved to roam in the quiet gardens of Gajona, and seated under his favorite cypress tree, he smiled happily as Achille sailed his boats on the deep blue waters of the lake. So calm and peaceful it was, that he decided never to go away again.

"Home is best!" he would sigh, stretching his long arms toward the sun-filled sky over his head.

But never could he be at peace for very long at a time. Visitors were always at his gate, begging for a few words with the master. The faintest whisper he could hear for a long distance, and when hushed voices would say, "Paganini? He is resting now; we cannot disturb him," he would leap from his bench, calling, "Giulia! Toni! Who comes? Bring them to me at once, here in the garden!"

Not far away from the Villa Gajona lived the Duchess of Parma at her splendid court. Hearing of the great honors that had been heaped upon her neighbor in other countries, she decided that something must be done for him in the land of his birth.

At once she set to work on her surprise, and her messengers sped throughout all Italy, inviting officials to the beautiful court for a very special event. Carefully they gave the Duchess warning: "We must keep the secret from the master until the very moment of his arrival at court."

My, what preparations there were at the palace! But by December all was in readiness, with the last chicken pie popped into the great oven.

The morning of the special day dawned in a blaze of golden sunshine, and happy after a long night's sleep, Paganini called for his simple breakfast.

"My chocolate, Toni!" he commanded. "And see that it is piping hot! Nothing more until tonight. I go this afternoon to my friend, the Duchess of Parma, to play a new composition

for her and a few others. Just a simple little gathering. "

It was well past midday when the master, in long black fur coat, started out in the carriage, his knees carefully wrapped in warm woolen blankets.

"We had better move right along, Giorgio," he called to the old driver. "The Duchess likes her guests to be on time."

But no sooner did they arrive at the main roadway than they came upon a line of carriages, as far as the eye could reach, winding slowly ahead of them.

"I must have made a mistake in the day!" Nicolo stood up in the carriage, peering anxiously this way and that. "The Duchess must be holding special court." He sat down with a sigh, pulling the blanket about him again. "Turn around, Giorgio. We had better go back home."

"Oh no, master, no!" the old coachman's words rushed out as he kept his eyes straight ahead. "No mistake! You tell Giorgio right day. Gid-ap, Bruno! Why you so pokey, Pino?" he urged the horses on.

How glad he was when they rounded the last curve safely and stood before the splendid villa of the Duchess of Parma!

"Your arm, Giorgio," called Nicolo, and slowly settled himself to the ground. "The old knees are getting a bit rusty. Father Time coming along, I reckon."

At the entrance leading into the great hall, the master

stopped abruptly, his heart beating fast. Singing as they came to meet him were beautiful young maidens in snowy garments, their arms filled with bright garlands. Encircling him gently, they drew him into the vast hall.

Four clear trumpet calls pealed in salute, and then, to the stately music of the orchestra, twenty officials in red velvet robes walked slowly toward him. The leader paused a moment, and from a shining casket drew a handsome golden chain, with gleaming pendant set in rare and precious jewels.

"Nicolo Paganini," said he, slowly, "In the name of Italy we come to bring you honor this day." With a solemn bow, he hung the kingly treasure about the neck of the master.

The orchestra struck up a martial air, and cries of "Paganini! Master! Master!" rang in deafening chorus as he was led to the chair of honor.

What a celebration there was, with speeches, dancing, and feasting lasting into the hours. At last, there was a hush as the master rose from his place at the head of the long table.

Pausing a moment, he took his beloved Stradivarius from its case and rested it lightly against his shoulder. Happy tears filled his dark eyes, and his voice trembled as he began to speak to the notable gathering around him.

"My countrymen," said he, "I will try to thank you for this great honor with which you have crowned my life. But what I feel is too deep for words. And so I must speak to you through music."

The golden tones of his lovely Concerto swept through the hall, the throbbing, haunting melody creeping into the hearts of his listeners, moving them as only his music could do.

The greatest master of the strings, that the world has ever known, had spoken, indeed. And the beautiful melodies of Nicolo Paganini are still stirring the hearts of men, wherever they are played, in his glorious songs of the strings.

Here you will find two delightful melodies from Paganini's first Concerto. If you have no violin at hand, just play the solo part on the piano. With someone accompanying you, a fine duet you will have.

ALLEGRO
(MUSIC APPRECIATION DISC 5 TRACK 40)

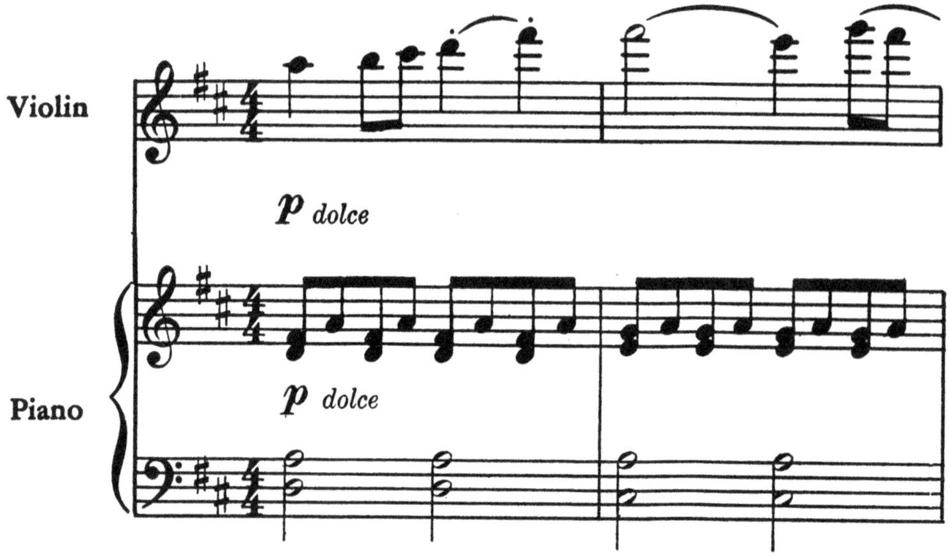

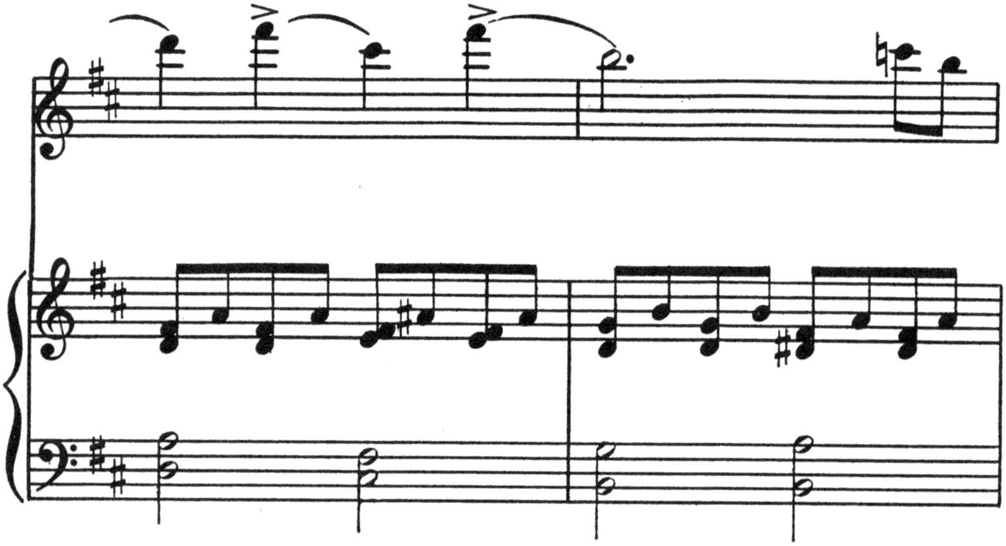

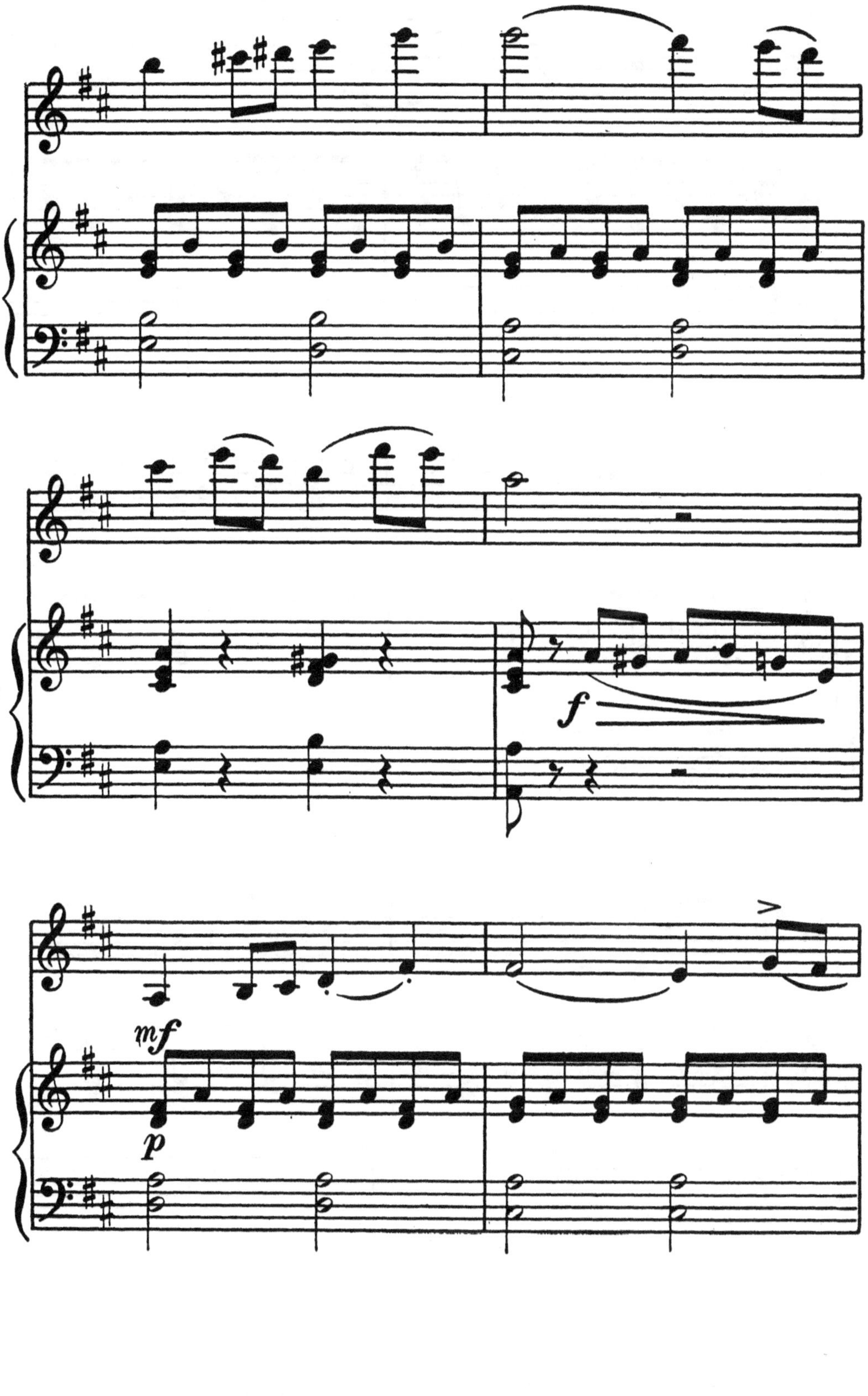
f
mf
p

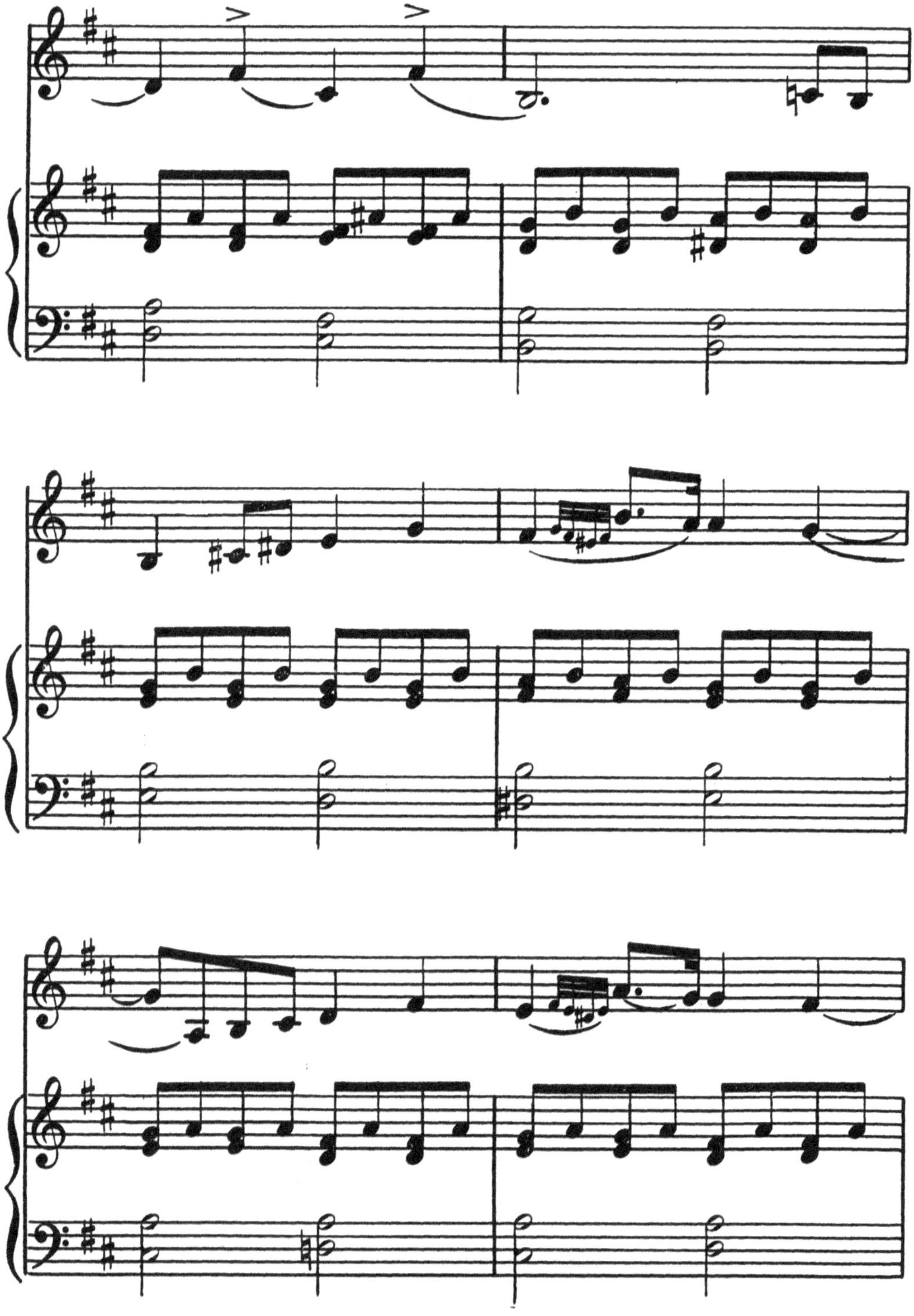

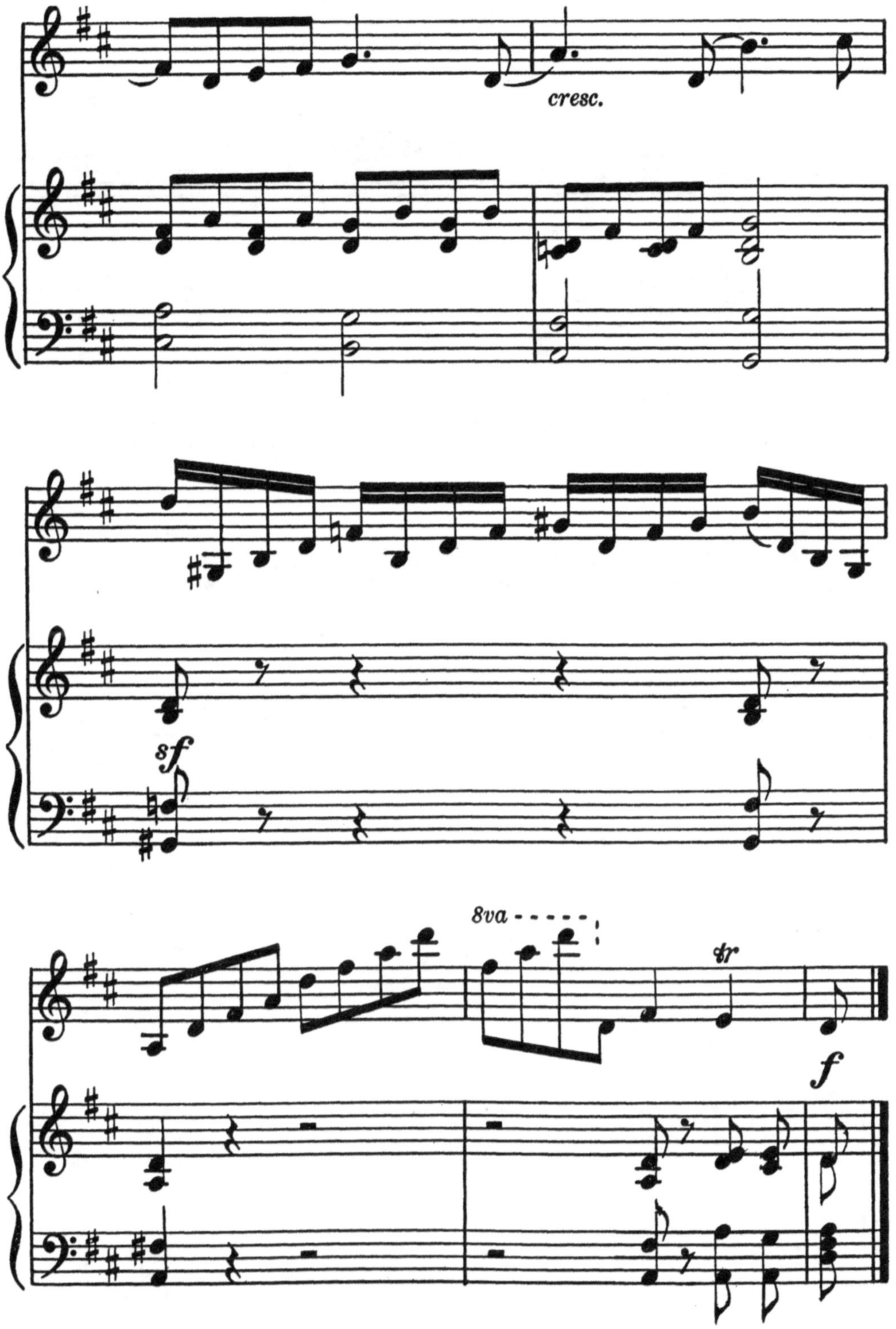
cresc.
sf
8va
tr
f

RONDO

(MUSIC APPRECIATION DISC 5 TRACK 41)

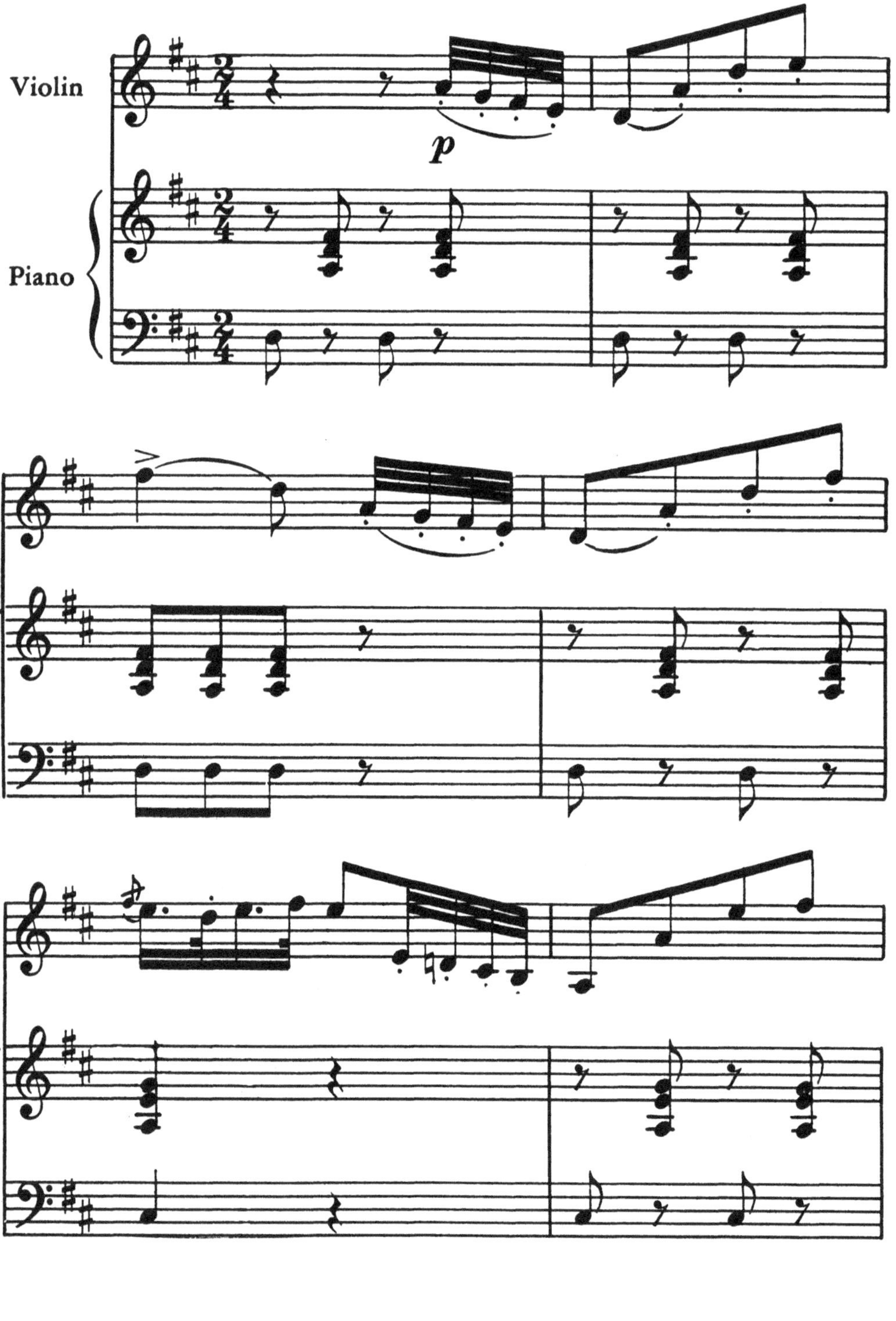

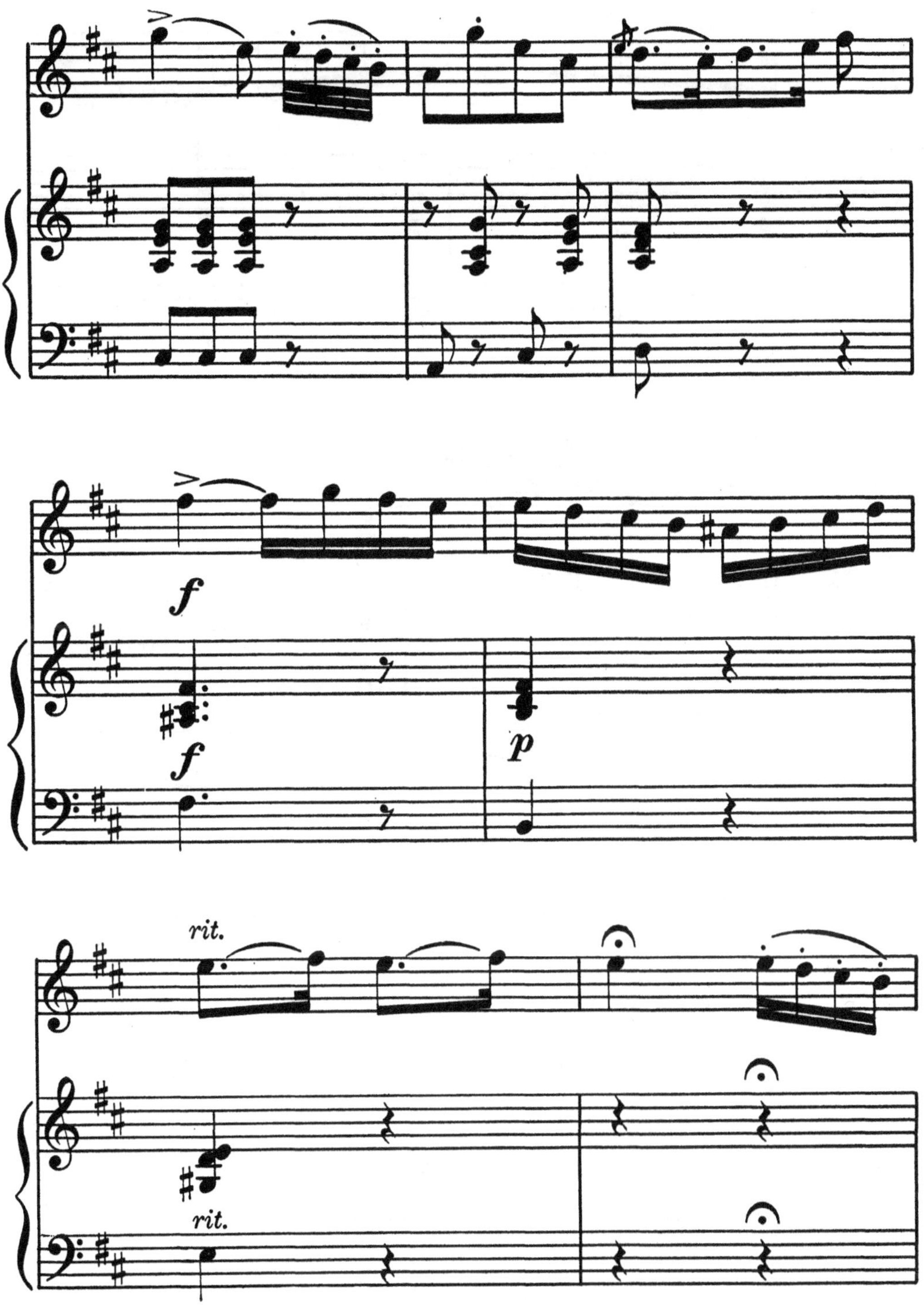
f
f
p
rit.
rit.

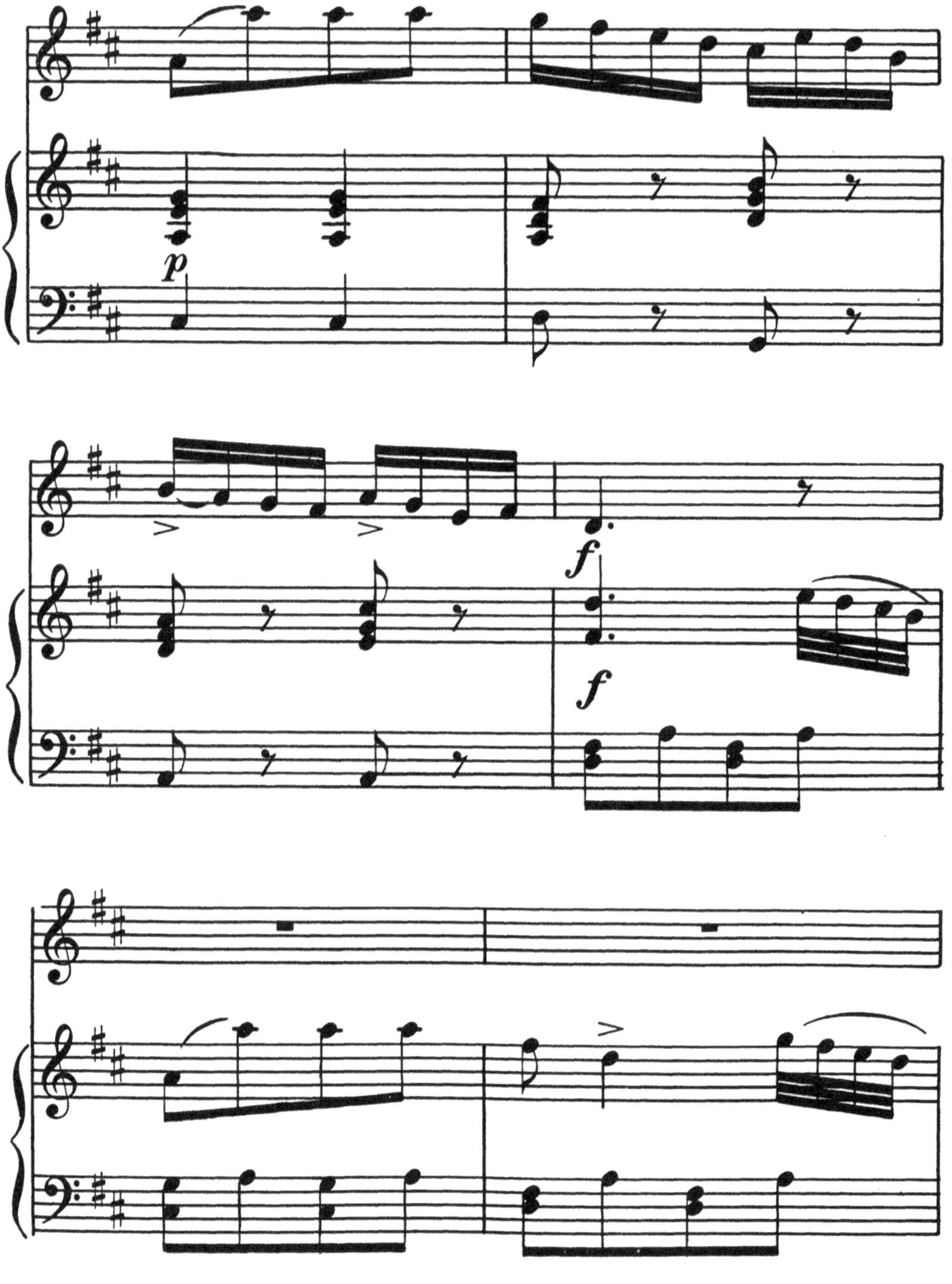
p
f
f

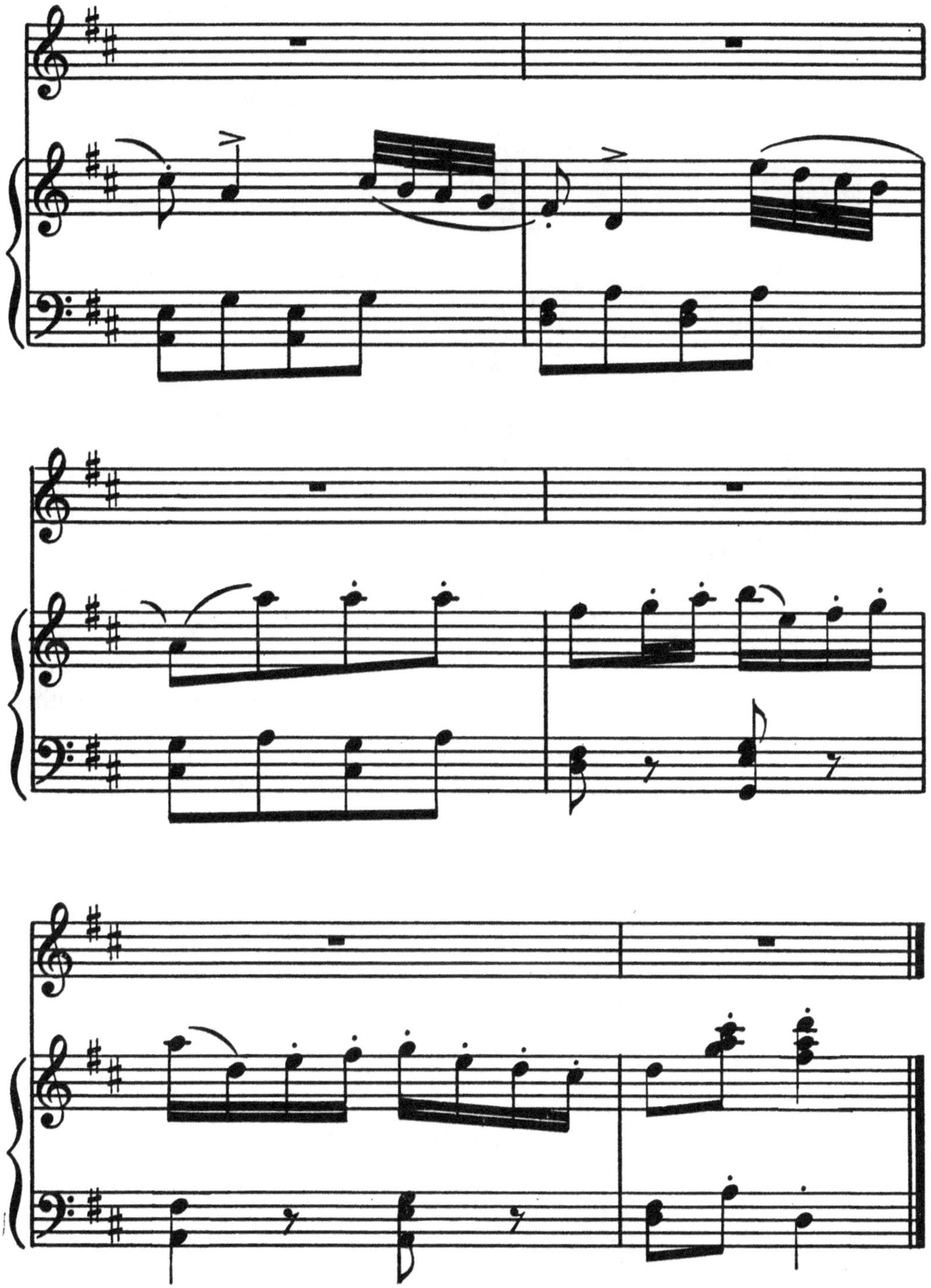

Paganini, Master of Strings is part of *Music Appreciation for the Elementary Grade: Book 1.*

Music Appreciation for the Elementary Grades will introduce children to seven different composers, dating from 1685 to 1828 (Bach, Handel, Haydn, Mozart, Beethoven, Paganini and Schubert). Each composer's childhood and adult life are vividly described in individual biographies. Every important incident is mentioned and every detail of the stories is true. Each book contains written music and delightful pictures throughout. It is more than the human side of these books that will make them live, for in the music the great masters breathe.

The Student Activity book includes a variety of hands-on activities such as: geography lessons, history lessons, recipes, instrument studies, music vocabulary, hand writing, musical facts of the Classical period, timelines, character trait studies, and so much more. Geared for a variety of learners— auditory, kinesthetic, visual, and just plain "active"—the Student Activity Book is an excellent companion to your reading experience.

<u>*Titles used in this curriculum are:*</u>
Sebastian Bach, The Boy from Thuringia
Handel at the Court of Kings
Joseph Haydn, The Merry Little Peasant
Mozart, The Wonder Boy
Ludwig Beethoven and the Chiming Tower Bells
Paganini, Master of Strings
Franz Schubert and His Merry Friends

For more information visit our website at www.Zeezok.com

Also available from Zeezok Publishing:

Music Appreciation: Book 2 for the Middle Grades (for grades 5 to 8) will introduce older children to seven different composers, dating from 1810 to 1908 (Chopin, Schumann, Wagner, Foster, Brahms, Tchaikovsky and MacDowell). Each composer's childhood and adult life are vividly described in individual biographies. Every important incident is mentioned and every detail of the stories is true. Each book contains written music and delightful pictures throughout. It is more than the human side of these books that will make them live, for in the music the great masters breathe.

The Student Book incorporates activities from across the curriculum and promotes an increased knowledge of and appreciation for classical music and the composers. Geared for a variety of learners—auditory, kinesthetic, visual, and just plain "active"—it is user-friendly for multi-age groups.

<u>Titles used in this curriculum are:</u>
Frederic Chopin, Early Years
Frederic Chopin, Later Years
Robert Schumann and Mascot Ziff
Adventures of Richard Wagner
Stephen Foster and His Little Dog Tray
The Young Brahms
The Story of Peter Tchaikovsky
Peter Tchaikovsky and the Nutcracker Ballet
Edward MacDowell and His Cabin in the Pines

For more information visit our website at www.Zeezok.com